Making Winter

For Andy, Evie, Rose, and Minnie,
and for the people who told me I could.

Making Winter

A Hygge-Inspired Guide for Surviving the Winter Months

Emma Mitchell

LARK
New York

LARK

New York

An Imprint of Sterling Publishing Co., Inc.
1166 Avenue of the Americas
New York, NY 10036

First published in the United Kingdom in 2017 by LOM Art, an imprint of Michael O'Mara Books Ltd., as *Making Winter: A Creative Guide to Surviving the Winter Months*

ISBN 978-1-4547-1056-1

Distributed in Canada by Sterling Publishing Co., Inc.
c/o Canadian Manda Group, 664 Annette Street
Toronto, Ontario, Canada M6S 2C8

For information about custom editions, special sales, and premium and corporate purchases, please contact Sterling Special Sales at 800-805-5489 or specialsales@sterlingpublishing.com.

Manufactured in China

2 4 6 8 10 9 7 5 3 1

sterlingpublishing.com
larkcrafts.com

Contents

Introduction

When the days start to shorten, I eye the trees warily. At the first yellowing leaf, I grumble inwardly; once the first branches are bare, I have an urge to swaddle myself in cozy clothing. In the bleak, incessant, slate gray days of midwinter, I peer at the sky with contempt and beadily watch the progress of the bulb shoots in the garden, egging them on until snowdrop time. Despite the presence of twinkly holiday celebrations, winter and I have a strained relationship. At best, I feel a little flat, but on very dreary days it makes me feel rather gloomy. Most years, as summer ends, I wish I were a grizzly bear and could eat all the cake and sandwiches in the picnic baskets of Yellowstone National Park, build up a pleasing layer of blubber, dig a large but snug hole, and go to sleep until the warmer weather draws me out. However, as a human being, it might be better to devise rather more sociable ways of embracing the colder months.

As the calendar shifts beyond autumn, the intensity of the sunlight available diminishes, as does the number of daylight hours. Sunlight has been shown to increase the levels of serotonin in the human nervous system, and if the sunlight is more intense, the effect is more pronounced. Serotonin is a neurotransmitter that directly affects the way we feel, and when bursts of it are released, we feel energized and our mood is lifted. This compound also influences our immune system. When its levels are lowered, it

can lead to feelings of sluggishness, listlessness, and anxiety, and can even affect the way in which we fight infections. During the winter months, we tend to spend more time indoors, which can lead to feeling rather Eeyore-ish. One way to fend off the dark forces is to gather as much light into the eyes—and serotonin into the neurons—as possible, by venturing out on walks.

Apart from the early brief blaze from dying leaves, the landscape looks rather drained of color once summer is over. The view from many windows becomes rather monochrome and shades of brown predominate. Green is less prevalent, and vibrant yellows, reds, and blues are almost nonexistent in the countryside and garden during winter. There is evidence that the

sight of yellow and red trigger mood-boosting changes in our neurotransmitters, so it is little wonder that many people experience less *joie de vivre* during the winter months.

Danish winters are especially long, with sunlight a rare commodity. But rather than experiencing a nationwide dingy gloom that might be expected in such a dark season, a sort of joy descends on the country during winter. *Hygge* (pronounced "hooga") is coziness, candlelight, nature, and meeting and eating with friends. In the last two years, it has become a bit of a trend, but there is a word to denote this feeling of cozy well-being in many countries. In Germany, *gemütlichkeit* means warmth, good cheer, and belonging. In Sweden, *gemytlig* is the

equivalent term, and the Italian word for this feeling, often used in winter, is *comodità*. There is no exact equivalent in English, but the feelings described by the words above are very familiar.

In recent years, I discovered that crafts and creativity helped replace the spring in my step and bring hygge into even the dreariest winter days. I started an online creative diary in 2008 and noticed that I felt somewhat less like an irascible hibernating bear on days when I had made something by hand, or baked, and that this effect was especially noticeable during winter. A year or two later, I learned to crochet, began to meet with friends once a week for needlearts and cake, and discovered that this was a source of solace in the long winter evenings. I found myself reaching for my crocheting on especially dreary days and that the repetitive, aesthetically pleasing process of making loops into stitches—which grew into soft blankets and scarves—absorbed my mind and lifted my mood. Baking a cake would bring a feeling of well-being that seemed to counter the flat fatigue that lurks during the grayest of days.

My anecdotal findings that creative activity can lift mood during winter are beginning to be supported by scientific research. It seems that needlearts can lead to a relaxation or meditation-like response similar to that induced by yoga,[2] and one study has shown that meditation increases the levels of dopamine, another neurotransmitter that is associated with elevated mood.[3] Knitting leads to improved feelings of well-being, and this effect is markedly increased when it takes place within a group of people.[4] Whipping up a pair of mittens could perhaps make the glass feel more full again.

Crocheting a Day-Glo, rainbow-striped onesie, climbing into it, and staring at your reflection in a mirror for four months may be a step too far, but the experience of visiting a yarn shop, with its beautiful skeins arranged in color-coordinated ombre groups, and the odd flash of vermilion or mustard, could be the vivid flowering meadow of the winter. Merino replaces marigolds. Thistle gives way to the softest pink alpaca. The colors of yarn, fabric, paint palettes, and printing ink and the creative process of making something with any of these, can replace the bursts of neurotransmitters released when you walk round a sun-drenched garden in full bloom in summer.

Making things during winter is a cunning strategy to embrace hygge during these dingier months. Combine the joy of baking, the thrill of a chocolate cake made in five minutes, the snugness of a homemade shawl and the deep satisfaction of meeting with friends to make some or all of the above, and the result is a delicious, cozy, baked, yarn-filled toolkit with which to tackle winter's onslaught.

This is a creative survival guide to winter, a means to embrace the drab days and fill them with wrist warmers and baked goodness. Grab your crochet hooks, yarn, and cocoa powder. Onwards into the cold…

1. http://www.theweathercompany.com/SAD%20research%20UK and http://www.independent.co.uk/life-style/health-and-families/health-news/seasonal-affective-disorder-1-in-3-people-suffer-from-sad-9814164.html
2. http://esource.dbs.ie/bitstream/handle/10788/1586/ba_croghan_c_2013.pdf?sequence=1
3. https://www.ncbi.nlm.nih.gov/pubmed/11958969
4. http://bjo.sagepub.com/content/76/2/50.abstract

Nature as Nurture

I find the urge to stay indoors during autumn and winter to be almost overwhelming. My instinct is to light a fire, swaddle myself in blankets and quilts, and feast on carbohydrates until the mercury starts to rise. However, as admirable as this plan is, hygge is more than just staying cozy beside a warm fireplace. It's also about appreciating the beauty of the natural world and enjoying the simple pleasures of feeling closer to nature. I know that venturing outdoors for an hour or two can lift the spirits and actually enhance a wintry nest.

It doesn't matter how low the light levels might be on a gray autumnal or winter's day. Allowing sunlight into your eyes by going outside for a walk increases serotonin in the brain, and a daily boost in its levels can help stave off the threat of feeling down. Similarly, a brisk stride around the park diminishes the stress hormone cortisol while boosting serotonin further. Simply being in a green space can alter the levels of mood-boosting neurotransmitters.[1] Add to this the plum blondies you may have taken with you and the soothing activities you'll be embarking upon when you return with the makings of a new craft project. Suddenly, the walk is transformed into something pleasantly medicinal, shifting your neurotransmitter dial towards joy.

Seed heads snipped from an obliging shrub, fallen cones, empty snail shells, and feathers picked up on a walk may not be as colorful and verdant as spring and summer nature finds, but they are beautiful and are especially cheery after holiday decorations have been taken down. Using field guides to identify and label what you've found is a gentle, meditative task and the small repetitive hand and eye movements made as you draw a feather or cluster of seeds can help

to increase levels of feel-good neurotransmitters even further. Research has shown that having plants in your home can boost your mood.[2] Small reminders of the nature walks you have taken may play the same role, so bring home any small treasures you may find.

If you live far away from a park, wood, or field, then a trip to a winter garden, where planting is designed to be at its best during the colder months, can be a reminder that all is not brown, dead, and crispy. Winter-flowering and berry-laden trees and shrubs such as *Viburnum bodnantense*, winter-flowering cherry (*Prunus subhirtella*), *Cotoneaster*, and *Callicarpa* can be laden with color even in midwinter and beyond. These gardens are often filled with the flame reds and oranges of dogwood (*Cornus*) stems and the frosty-looking thorny branches of ornamental blackberries.

Casting your eyes over this color and growth, followed by a large scone with jam and cream or a slab of brownie in the tearoom, will lead to winter flower and cake-based contentment.

1. http://www.motherearthnews.com/nature-and-environment/ importance-of-nature-zm0z15djzcom and http://www.bbc. co.uk/news/science-environment-25682368 and http://www. newyorker.com/tech/elements/what-is-a-tree-worth
2. http://krex.k-state.edu/dspace/handle/2097/227

Preserving Autumn Flora

In autumn and early winter, chlorophyll, the green pigment within leaves, is broken down, and the red and yellow pigments called anthocyanins and carotenoids that are present all year round are unmasked. The leaves of some species such as maples, Boston ivy, and cherry trees are jewel-like and beautiful, and I always have a strong urge to gather them from the ground and bring them home. The problem is that they dry up quickly and become crispy or begin to decay. I've often wondered about capturing the color of those leaves somehow: a way of putting them into suspended animation for later in the winter, when outdoor natural color is scarce.

Last year, I tried preserving leaves and berries in glycerin for the first time. They remained pliable and shiny, and didn't fade or dry: leafy joy! When certain large flowers, autumn leaves, or berries are submerged in a glycerin solution, some of the water in their cells is replaced by glycerin molecules, which remain in the cells, preventing further drying or loss of pigment. This method may take several days, but the effort required is minimal, and it can result in a collection of beautifully preserved plant materials for use in creative projects.

Materials

Your chosen leaves, berries, or flowers
Glycerin (found at most drugstores)
Water
Baking sheets, roasting pans, or a tall jug
A couple of pebbles and string or twine (if preserving large flowers or berry clusters)

Leaves to Look Out For
Boston ivy
Maple (including field maple)
Birch
Ivy
Cotoneaster
Some varieties of cherry trees

Note: You can use this method to preserve several leaves attached to one twig or a slender branch from species like birch and field maple, whose leaves are relatively small. Large flowers such as hydrangeas and slender branches with berries such as hawthorn or rosehip can also be preserved in this way.

Step by Step

1 Make a solution of 1 part glycerin to 2 parts water.

2 To preserve individual leaves and pliable stems or branches, pour the glycerin solution into a large roasting pan, submerge the stems and leaves, and find a way to keep them submerged in the solution. Placing a baking tray on top of the stems and leaves works well.

3 To preserve large flowers such as hydrangeas or clusters of berries, pour your glycerin solution into a jug, tie a pebble or two to the base of the stem or berry cluster with string or twine, and lower into the liquid. The pebble(s) will ensure that your foraged treasure will stay submerged during the preservation time.

4 Leave your leaves, berries, and flowers in their solution for at least two days but no more than four.

5 Remove your finds from the glycerin solution, rinse them briefly in water, then dry them by blotting them with paper towels or leave them out overnight at room temperature.

6 That's it! Put your leaves in a vase (don't add water) or use them in creative projects. They last an incredibly long time. Mine from last autumn are still going strong.

Tips

You could use the leaves to trim natural wreaths (see page 76 for details), add them to nature collections you might be making through the winter, or sketch or paint them (see page 33 and page 96).

Fennel Cowl

If you're a beginner and would like to learn the basic crochet stitches, you can find full instructions on my website: silverpebble.net.

As autumn approaches, umbellifer seed heads are a common sight in Fenland hedgerows. Umbellifers are wildflower annuals with flowers shaped like tiny upturned umbrellas, and include cow parsley, wild carrot (Queen Anne's lace), wild fennel, and pignut.

This cowl pattern uses clusters of treble crochet stitches to form an umbellifer-like motif. It echoes the fennel flower heads I see in the woods, behind our cottage that appear in huge drifts of exquisite lacy blooms in spring and summer. This cowl is perfect for wearing out on cold days, as the fabric formed is dense and will keep out the chill. I have used chunky Malabrigo Mecha in Polar Morn, a beautiful gray-blue colorway that evokes frozen ponds and snow-laden clouds.

Materials

Malabrigo Mecha (100% Superwash Merino Wool; 3.5 ounces/100 g = 142 yards/130 m): 1 skein in #009 Polar Morn or approximately 142 yards/130 m of chunky weight yarn
6 mm (size J-10) crochet hook
Scissors
Yarn needle for weaving in ends

Abbreviations & Definitions

ch chain
sk skip
sp space
sl st slip stitch
sc singel crochet
dc double crochet
tr treble crochet
yo yarn over
st/s stitch/es
hdc half double crochet: yo, insert hook, yo, pull through, yo, pull through all 3 loops on hook
shell work 9 tr in one stitch

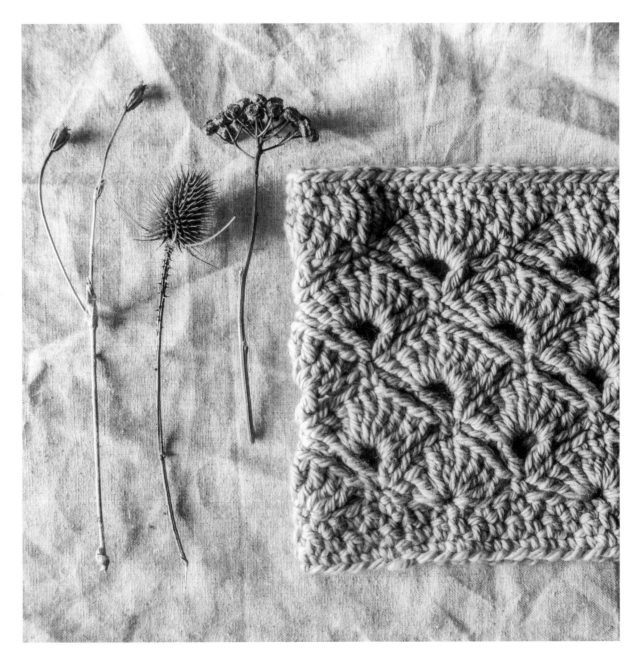

Pattern

To begin, work a loose foundation chain of 80 stitches. Join your chain with a sl st to work in the round, being careful not to twist the chain.

Round 1: ch 1 (does not count as st throughout), sc in each st to end, join with a sl st in first sc.

Round 2: ch 1, *sc 1, dc 1; repeat from * to end, join with a sl st in first sc.

Round 3: ch 1, *dc 1, sc 1; repeat from * to end, join with a sl st in first dc.

Round 4: ch 1, *sc 1, sk 3 sts, shell in next st, sk 3 sts; repeat from * 9 more times, join with a sl st in first sc.

Round 5: ch 4, tr 1 in first sc (at base of ch 4), *ch 3, sc 1 in 5th tr of shell, ch 3, (tr 1, ch 1, tr 1) in next sc; repeat from * 8 more times, ch 3, sc in 5th tr, do not sl st but continue to Round 6.

Round 6: Make shell in space between 4 ch and first tr of Round 5, sc in next sc, *shell in next 1 ch sp, sc in next sc; repeat from * 8 more times, do not sl st but begin next round after working final sc.

Rounds 7–12: Repeat Rounds 5 and 6. (Note: The beginning of round will shift to the right as you work.)

Round 13: ch 4 (counts as 1 tr), sk st at base of ch, tr 1, dc 1, hdc 1, *sc3, hdc 1, dc 1, tr 3, dc 1, hdc 1; repeat from * 8 more times, sc 3, hdc 1, dc 1, tr 1, join with a sl st to top of 4 ch.

Round 14: ch 1, sc in each st to end, join with a sl st in first sc. Fasten off and weave in ends.

Plum and Orange Blondies

When I emerge from the house during winter, I'm always surprised by how good it feels. Nestling by an open fire is all very well, but even when there's an incessant drizzle wafting drearily from the sky, being outdoors can be uplifting. If you're off on a walk, though, a day with that almost transparent, liquid winter sunshine is the best choice. Taking a piece or two of something delicious to eat on the way will make the walk even lovelier. Imagine stopping for a few minutes in the clearing of a wood and eating one of these fruity, citrus-flavored blondies while sitting on a bench in the winter sunshine. Sunshine boosts mood and so do carbohydrates, especially when laced with plums steeped in sloe gin and orange. It's a recipe to put a spring in your step.

Ingredients

¾ cup (180 g) plus 2 teaspoons
   light brown sugar
4 large eggs
1 cup (225 g) butter, melted
1¼ cups (150 g) all-purpose flour
Zest of 1 orange
Pinch of salt
3 plums, pitted and chopped
   into ½-inch (1-cm) cubes
2 tablespoon sloe gin (optional)
2 teaspoons ground ginger (optional)

Makes 8–12 pieces

Step by Step

1 Line an 8-inch (20-cm) square or 8 x 12-inch (20 x 30-cm) rectangular baking pan with parchment paper and preheat your oven to 350°F (180°C).

2 If you have a little extra time, place your chopped plums in a saucepan with the sloe gin and 2 teaspoons sugar. Bring the mixture to a simmer for about a minute, stirring gently. This allows the gin to infuse into the plums, the sugar to dissolve, and (some of) the alcohol to evaporate. Drain the sloe gin syrup into a cup. If time is tight, or alcohol isn't your thing, the chopped plums will still taste delicious in the blondies without their gin treatment.

3 Place the sugar and eggs in a large bowl and whisk together for 3 minutes until the mixture is light and voluminous.

4 Carefully pour the melted butter into the mixture while continuing to whisk. Ensure that the butter is well combined before moving on to the next step.

5 Fold in the flour, baking powder, orange zest, and salt, then whisk again to add a little more air.

6 Add the plums and ginger (if using) and fold into the mixture carefully to distribute them evenly.

7 Pour the mixture into the lined pan and shake gently to level it. Then, if you'd like to add decoration, you can add slices of plum to the top. Bake for 25–30 minutes or until a toothpick inserted into the blondies comes out clean.

8 Allow the blondies to cool, cut into squares, and either take with you on a walk or serve with a dollop of whipped cream and a drizzle of the sloe gin syrup on top for a fancy-ish dessert. Alternatively, save the small glass of plum-infused sloe gin and enjoy it in private.

Silver Fossil Pendant

Silver clay is an astonishing substance made from the finely ground silver recovered from the printed circuit boards inside broken electrical devices. A compound containing cotton fiber is used to bind the clay together. It can be used to capture the tiniest details from nature by pressing leaves, silicone molds made from fossils, seedpods, or acorns into its surface. No expensive or high-tech equipment is required to make jewelry from silver; a gas hob or camping stove, a piece of steel wool, metal polishing pads, and a small brush are all that is needed to begin at home. The basic tools and materials aren't very expensive, and you can acquire these from craft stores or online.

There is a moment after you have just fired your pendant, plunged it into water to cool it, and begun to polish off the silver oxide, when many people gasp. I've even witnessed some becoming a little tearful at this point. A piece of rather drab, unpromising-looking clay is transformed into a piece of pure silver, and a beautiful piece of jewelry. It's a modern version of alchemy.

Materials

For the pendant:

2–4 grams silver clay (such as Art Clay Silver 650 Slow Dry)
Sharp straight edge
Small plastic rolling pin (a thick marker pen also works well)
Plain, flat glazed tile
Drop of cooking oil
Wax paper
Selection of leaves
1 head pin
Circular or leaf-shaped cookie cutter, 1 inch (2–3 cm) in diameter
Baby wipe or piece of dampened paper towel, folded several times
Long tweezers
Gas hob or camping stove
Wire gauze

For the finish:

Small steel or brass wire brush
Polishing paper
Old aluminium knitting needle for burnishing (optional)
A solution of bleach, 1 part bleach and 3 parts water (optional)
Small amount of water in a saucer

For the necklace:

1 3- or 4-gauge silver-plated or sterling silver jump ring
Silver-plated or sterling silver fine chain necklace
Pliers

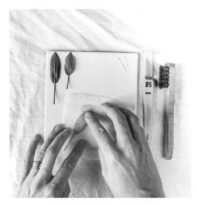  

Step by Step

1 Ensure your tile is clean and dry and then rub a small drop of oil onto it. This will prevent your silver clay from sticking to the surface. Cut a piece of wax paper around 4-inch (10-cm) square.

2 Use your knife to cut a ½ x ½ inch (1 cm x 1 cm) piece of clay and place it on your oiled surface. Rewrap the remainder of your clay carefully in its original packaging to keep for your next project.

3 Roll out your piece of silver clay into a circular shape as evenly as you can until it is just bigger than 1 inch (2 cm) in diameter. Try not to roll it thinner than ¹⁄₁₆ inch (1.6 mm) or your pendant will be very fragile at the smoothing stage.

4 Place the reverse side of your leaf onto the silver clay, ensuring its stalk extends beyond the edge of the rolled-out clay a little—this will make it easier to remove the leaf from the clay later. Carefully, place your wax paper on top of it, making sure you don't shift the leaf from its position. Rub the leaf gently through the wax paper with the pad of your finger, especially along the leaf's central vein, to impress the detail of the veins into the clay.

5 Lift the wax paper off the clay, carefully grasp the end of the leaf stalk, and peel the leaf away from the clay. If you prefer the outline of your pendant to remain organic and just as you rolled it out, then go on to step 6. If you'd rather have a perfectly circular pendant, then press a cookie cutter into the clay in your chosen position, hold the cutter in place, and use your knife to remove the uneven edges. Roll the leftover pieces into a ball and place them back into your silver clay package to use another time.

6 Poke your head pin into the silver clay around ⅛ inch (2–3 mm) down from the top of your fossil pendant using the ball end. Ensure the head pin is pressed right down through the clay to the hard surface beneath. Move the wire end of the head pin in tiny circles to open the hole up. This creates a space for your jump ring, which will allow you to hang your pendant from your chain.

7 Use the pad of your finger to gently and carefully flatten any raised areas around the jump ring hole you have made.

Leaves to Look Out For

Leaves with prominent veins make the best fossil pendants. Sage and salvias usually keep some leaves during winter, as do primulas and primroses, and on the backs of their leaves are beautiful filigree veins that lend themselves perfectly to this project. Alpine thyme, ferns, heathers, and fir species with small needles are also excellent options.

8 Put your pendant, still attached to its tile, into the oven at 175°F (80°C) for 15–20 minutes. This will remove all the moisture from your pendant, preventing any water in your design from boiling and ruining its surface when you fire it. Allow it to cool.

9 After drying, the fossil pendant should detach easily from the tile. Hold it very carefully, supporting the edge with your fingers (it can be rather brittle at this stage, like a very thin cookie). Use the folded baby wipe or damp paper towel to remove any ragged or sharp pieces from around

the edge. Smooth the rough pieces of clay away gently. If too much pressure or force is applied to the dry clay at this stage, it can snap or split.

10 Hold the pendant up to a light and ensure that you can see through the hole you have made near the top. If not, place it on a hard surface and very carefully use the head pin to open the hole a little more.

11 Place your wire gauze over one of the hobs of your gas cooker or on your camping stove. Light the gas, turn it up to its highest level, and let the gauze heat up until one or more areas become red hot.

12 Carefully use your tweezers to place the pendant on one of the red-hot areas of the gauze. Take care when placing the pendant onto the gauze for firing and when quenching as it will be very hot.

13 Watch carefully—a wisp of smoke followed by a flame will rise up from your pendant. This flame is from the burning cotton and paper fibers within the clay. Do not turn the gas flame off. Once the flame from your pendant has died down, leave the gas flame burning beneath your pendant for another 3–5 minutes before turning it off. This ensures that all the cotton fibers burn away completely, leaving pure silver.

14 Let the pendant cool for 5 minutes on the gauze. It should look matte white—this is the silver oxide on the surface. Hold your pendant

firmly and use your wire brush to polish the oxide away reveal the silver underneath. (This is a very exciting moment!) Be persistent with your brush. The pendant is now made of silver and no longer fragile—you don't have to be careful.

15 You can leave your pendant with a matte, brushed silver finish, or you can use your polishing paper to shine the surface.

16 Experiment with burnishing by using the edge of an old aluminium knitting needle to create areas of very high shine that contrast well with the matte finish.

17 If you'd like to highlight the tiny details of your pendant even further, then immerse it in the bleach solution for 1–2 minutes. Rinse in your saucer of water and repeat the polishing and burnishing process in steps 15 and 16.

18 Use your pliers to open the silver jump ring, slip the ring through the hole you made at the top of your pendant, and thread your necklace or bracelet chain through the ring. Close the jump ring using your pliers.

19 That's it—your silver fossil is finished. Try on your necklace and get ready to bask in the inevitable slew of compliments.

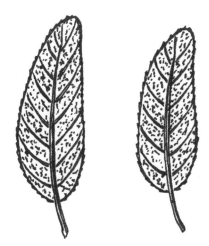

Tips

If the clay begins to dry out a little while you are making your pendant, don't worry. Moisten your finger with a droplet of water and dab the clay. It should become soft again and revitalize the surface. If you discover that the clay has dried out while in storage, then place it in a small resealable bag, add a couple of drops of water, and knead the water into the clay. Continue kneading until the clay is uniformly soft (this may take up to 20 minutes) and then reuse.

Nature Diaries

lychnis

Streptopelia

Hedera

As winter progresses, bright sunlight becomes more scarce, and taking regular walks, even short ones of just ten or fifteen minutes, really can lift your mood. Endorphins will be released as a result of the gentle exercise and serotonin levels will rise due to the exposure to sunlight, even if that light is lurking stubbornly behind a cloud. I have spent far too many days covalently bonded to my laptop and sofa on wintry days, and I can vouch for the fact that a brief constitutional can help to banish the urge to channel a hibernating dormouse. Plus, you might see a weasel while you're out there.

One way to stop regular walks from feeling like part of a very worthy Victorian health regime is to record what you see while you're outdoors. Taking photographs on your phone is an excellent way to mark and observe the subtle changes that occur as winter progresses. Writing down and even drawing what you find each week helps to transform a walk from an obligation, easily avoided, into something to savor. Alternatively, you could make a nature collection by arranging and labelling your finds. This practice harks back to the collections of nineteenth-century naturalists and their cabinets of curiosity. For me, it echoes the displays in my favorite museums, where the faded copperplate labels, many written in the nineteenth and early twentieth centuries, are as beautiful as the exhibits themselves.

I remember one dank December day last year when I wrenched myself away from the coziness of our cottage. I

Salix caprea

Cepaea nemoralis

Acer pseudoplatanus

walked to the edge of the village, where there is a tiny bridge over a Roman lode, a canal-like waterway that was used to travel between Ely and the surrounding settlements by boat and barge. The sycamore branches were bare, and I stood for a few minutes looking at the patterns they made against the gray sky. Then, at the corner of my vision, I saw a quick flurry of animal movement on the opposite bank of the lode. I assumed it was a cat or perhaps a rat, but as my eyes shifted focus from sky to ground, I realized that the movement was snaking and that the animal was long, slender and very quick. It was a weasel and it seemed to writhe through the tired winter foliage on the lode bank as it made its way under the bridge. I had only ever seen a weasel a few times in my life and never at such close quarters. I was so glad that I'd parted from

the soft furnishings and come on my walk. I felt privileged to have seen this animal.

Most of the nature observations I make on my winter walks are more mundane than watching a weasel scamper among ivy, but they are no less uplifting. I often have to drive across the Fens to pick up silver clay supplies from a neighboring village. The road is lined with young oak trees, and in October, the acorns begin to ripen and fall. Last year, my eldest daughter and I set about collecting acorns for my workshops (I teach people how to cast them in silver). The range of colors of the acorns we found was astonishing— from almost yellow and through all the browns you could conceive of to a bright acid green. I brought them home and recorded them on Instagram, which has, since 2015, become a sort of nature journal for me.

It's not too late to learn a little more about the wild birds, plants, and specimens we may discover on a walk. Early winter is a good time to begin—there will still be the bright leaves of cherry trees, jewel-like rose hips and berries, umbellifer seed heads, acorns, molted feathers, and the cones of alder, larch, and pine trees to find. A field guide or two will help you to identify species of land snails and to tell whether you have found a cow parsley or hogweed seed head. (Giant hogweed causes skin burns; avoid seed heads that are over six feet or 1.8 meters tall and as big as a cat.) Getting outside, recording what you see, bringing home small finds, and drawing and annotating them can be part of an uplifting and soothing daily project that lasts throughout the winter.

Craft Night

For many, a period of self-deprivation and almost punishment for the indulgences of the holidays descends in the New Year. Thoughts turn to sneakers and the juice squeezed from a vegetable. These have their merits, but Danes have little time for austere regimes in winter. A crucial part of a hygge approach to winter is kindness to oneself—finding the means to brighten winter days by seeking comfort, good company, and delicious food. If that food contains butter and sugar and is deep-fried to enhance its allure, then so much the better. A little indulgence is part of the Scandinavian winter plan.

In recent winters, there has been a permanent fixture in my planner every Thursday night. I meet with two friends, and we make things together. Essential ingredients for this small but excellent event are an open fire; a warming, usually hedgerow-based liqueur; refined carbohydrates (usually cake); and the particular yarn-based or sewing project each of us is working on at the time. We often bring slippers and sometimes pajama bottoms to one another's houses, and nestling under blankets is a regular occurrence. The most joyous part of craft night, though, is the companionship of these two excellent women. For us, making things by hand is not a passing fad—it's as essential as eating. Without it, life is rather drab. That satisfied feeling of donning your latest hat and knowing that you made it yourself is enhanced when you show it to friends who know just how much effort went into it.

I believe that these positive feelings come from the evolutionary benefits of being able to fashion clothing out of animal skins, spin fleece into yarn, and knit or weave blankets and garments. People who were skilled at sewing, weaving, knitting,

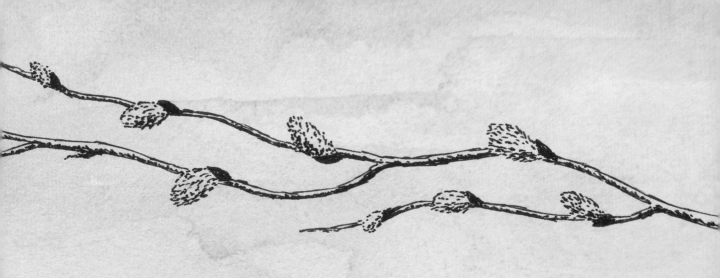

weapon-making, carving, or shelter-building were more likely to survive the colder weather. Our need for protection against the elements may have operated as a sort of natural selection for crafting skills, and it is likely that most modern human beings still have these innate abilities. The feelings of well-being that are experienced when we make a hat or even a pile of logs for the fire are inherited from our ancestors. Equally, the very basis of our success as a species is connected with our ability to cooperate and share our collective knowledge. It is no wonder to me that when several people gather together to make something in a group there is an extra feeling of rightness and well-being.

If getting together with friends is tricky for you, there are many craft communities online that you can join: knit-alongs and crochet-alongs happen regularly in Ravelry groups or on blogs. I've included as many seasonal handmade projects in this book as I could fit between the covers, and I hope that making them alone on a cold Saturday afternoon with the radio on might make a midwinter day lovelier. However, many of them could also be made with pals in close proximity to cake, conversation, and even more comfort and cheer on dingy evenings.

Pantile Shawl

When I glance out of our bedroom window in November, I notice the swag-like patterns made by the 200-year-old interlocking terracotta tiles (known as pantiles) on the roof of a cottage across the village green. Sometimes, winter brings out the details of buildings that may be overshadowed by trees and flowers during the warmer months. I confess that I thought of Florentine as well as Fenland roof tiles when I designed this shawl (sometimes my mind wanders to Tuscany on dreary afternoons).

The stitch I have used in this shawl uses stretches of chain stitches and little picot loops to create an attractive open trellis- or tile-like pattern, but the holes are not so big as to prevent the fabric from keeping you warm on a wintry walk. Despite its intricate look, the pattern is deceptively simple. Beginners can tackle it without worrying about the calculus-like complexity of so many shawl patterns.

Perhaps my favorite element of this pattern is its meditative repetition. Once you have crocheted the simple stitches a few times, your fingers will become familiar with it, and a finger-yarn-brain autopilot takes over. It's a perfect pattern to make with friends on craft night, as you can discuss the historical accuracy of the latest period TV show while working this up.

Materials

Madelinetosh Home Yarn (100% Superwash Merion Wool; 3.5 ounces/100 g = 110 yards/224 m): 4 skeins in Smokestack or approximately 440 yards/896 m of chunky weight yarn (5)
8 mm (size L-11) crochet hook
Scissors
Yarn needle for weaving in ends

Abbreviations

ch chain
sl st slip stitch
sc single crochet
picot 3 ch, 1 sl st in sc just made

If you're a beginner and would like to learn the basic crochet stitches, you can find full instructions on my website: silverpebble.net.

Pattern

To begin, create a foundation chain with a multiple of 4 stitches plus 4. For example, I made a foundation chain of 164. Drape this foundation chain around your shoulders and add multiples of 4 until it is the length you want.

Row 1: 1 sc in 8th ch from hook, picot, *7 ch, skip 3 ch, 1 sc in next ch, 3 ch, picot,
repeat from * ending 1 sc in last ch. Turn.
Row 2: 7 ch, skip first 3 ch, *1 sc in next ch (4th of 7 ch), picot, 7 ch, skip [3 ch, next sc, picot, 3 ch],
repeat from * ending 1 sc in 4th of 7 ch. Turn.
Repeat Row 2 ending: 1 sc in 4th of 7 ch.

Continue adding rows to the shawl until it is your preferred width. I made 20 rows after the initial foundation chain.
To finish: turn, 7 ch, skip 3 ch, sc in next ch, picot, fasten off, and weave in ends.

Note: You can also use this pattern to make a beautiful scarf using a shorter foundation chain and fewer rows. For a denser shawl with smaller gaps, use Aran or worsted weight yarn and a 5 mm (size H-8) or 6 mm (size J-10) crochet hook.

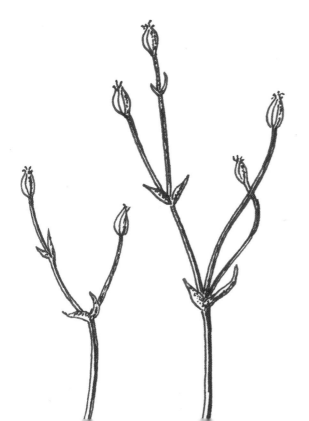

Apple and Caramel Chelsea Buns

These buns are the British version of a Danish pastry and were first invented in the Old Chelsea Bun House in London some time during the 1700s. The dough is enriched and often flavored with lemon or spices; the classic filling is made with butter, brown sugar, and dried fruits. Once baked, they're glazed to make glistening spirals of light bread dough drenched in toffee flavor icing.

My recipe takes advantage of the availability of baking apples during the colder months. There's something about the sharp yet sweet flavor that I associate with comfort and with winter. Stewed apple, sometimes with custard, was a regular dessert when I was small. Here, the pairing of soft tangy apple with light bread dough and caramel is reassuring, filling, and best eaten with a pot of tea.

This is not a speedy recipe. Once you decide to reach for the ingredients, it will be two hours or so before you can demolish your first bun—but the slowness of the process and the tantalizing anticipation is part of its joy. I find kneading and cutting buns from a batch of risen dough as soothing as making stitches with yarn. Between the gentle bursts of baking activity required to conjure your batch of appley spirals,

I recommend retreating back into a book, a crochet project, or a good film. It's a cozy Sunday recipe that lends itself to a slower pace. It is a duvet for your taste buds—hygge in a bun.

Ingredients

For the dough:
3 tablespoons (42 g) butter
¾ cup (180 g) milk
4 cups (500 g) bread flour
2¼ teaspoons instant yeast
1 teaspoon salt
1 egg

For the apple caramel filling:
2 large baking apples, peeled and grated
⅓ cup (75g) brown sugar
4 tablespoons (57g) butter, melted
1 tablespoon golden syrup or corn syrup
Lemon zest

For the glaze:
8 tablespoons milk
6 tablespoons golden syrup or corn syrup*
Good pinch of salt

*Note: Grease the tablespoon before measuring the syrup, and it'll slip off the spoon much more easily.

Makes 12 buns

Step by Step

1 Grease a 9-inch (23 cm) cake pan or 9 x 9-inch (23 x 23-cm) square baking pan generously and set aside.

2 Warm the butter and milk in a pan until the butter is just starting to melt. Then take it off the heat and let it cool while you measure out your dry ingredients. If the mixture is too warm, it may kill some of your yeast and impede the rise of your buns.

3 Put the flour, salt, and yeast into a bowl. Make a well in the center of the dry ingredients, break the egg into it, and pour in the butter mixture. Stir with a table knife until all the ingredients come together into a uniform, sticky dough.

4 Knead the dough on a floured surface for 10 minutes.

5 Leave the dough to rise in a covered, lightly greased bowl in a warm place for an hour. This is the first rise.

6 Once you've grated your apples, put them in a sieve and press them with a wooden spoon to remove some of the juice.

7 Put the grated apple in a bowl, add all the other ingredients for your filling, and mix together.

8 Once the dough has doubled in size, roll it into a rough rectangle about 10 x 16 inches (25 x 40 cm), spread your filling on to its surface leaving a 1-inch (2-cm) space along the long edge furthest away from you. Roll the rectangle into a log shape by starting at the long edge nearest you and rolling towards the far edge. Pinch the edge of the dough and the main body of the log together to prevent the filling from leaking out.

9 Cut your log of dough into quarters. Cut each quarter into three pieces to make twelve buns about 1–2 inches (3–4 cm) wide. Place the buns into your baking tin next to each other. If you push them together just a little, the final proof will result in a pleasing square-ish shape with a spiral of filling: the classic Chelsea bun design.

10 Place the scraps of the dough into the pan to bake with the buns (just tuck them in around the edge). They'll be hard after baking, but are very good dipped in a mug of tea or coffee.

11 Leave your buns to rise in their pan for half an hour. This is the final proof. Meanwhile, preheat your oven to 360°F (180°C).

12 Bake your buns for 30–45 minutes or until they are a deep golden brown. I cover mine with foil after 15–20 minutes or so, as they brown quite quickly in my oven.

13 While they're baking, make the glaze: simply put the milk, salt, and syrup into a saucepan, bring to a boil, and turn down the heat. Stirring constantly, allow the mixture to simmer very gently on low heat for 2 minutes to thicken slightly. Remove from heat and keep stirring as the glaze can sometimes separate.

14 Remove your buns from the oven and pour the glaze over the top while they're still warm. The glaze will soak into the dough and seep underneath the buns to form a delicious sweet-yet-sharp caramel sauce. Serve to friends or loved ones in triumph, with large mugs of tea, coffee, or hot chocolate. Alternatively, hoard them all for yourself and eat them when everyone's out.

Homemade Fire Lighters

During winter, lighting candles or a fire at dusk is a reassuring ritual that harks back to our ancestors. Several thousand years ago, a fire would have been the only source of light in winter, and I believe that the feeling of home and relief triggered by bringing light into a dark afternoon or early evening has its roots in human history.

A few minutes spent lighting candles or tea lights and placing them around your living room each evening really can lift a wintry mood—I speak from experience. If you're lucky enough to have an open fire, then lighting it can be part of this ancient routine. These homemade fire lighters can bring you slightly closer to the tinderboxes of previous centuries, when making and maintaining a flame required a certain amount of craft and resourcefulness. I have tested them, and they not only burn for several minutes, but they also add a subtle scent to a room if essential oil or dried orange peel is used to make them. A bag of the scented versions of these fire lighters make a lovely present and the plain versions can also be used to light bonfires, campfires, fire baskets, or barbecues.

Materials

1½ ounces (43 g) wax
A few drops of essential oil (optional)
Saucepan of boiling water
Heatproof bowl with a diameter larger
  than that of your saucepan
Cotton balls
Parchment paper
Tongs or tweezers
Garden twine cut into 12-inch
  (30-cm) lengths (1 length of
  twine for each firelighter)
Dry twigs or pieces of dried
  orange peel (optional)
Matches

Makes about 15 to 20 fire lighters

Note: Most garden twines are treated with paraffin or something similar to prevent them from rotting while outdoors. Sniff the twine before you buy it. If it smells like paraffin, it's perfect for this project.

Step by Step

1 Melt the wax in the heatproof bowl by placing the bowl over a pan of boiling water. At this point, you can add a drop or two of your favorite essential oil into the wax, if you like.

2 Fluff up the cotton balls a little to ensure there are lots of protruding fibers—these will be the "tinder" that catches the flame from the match and carries it to the wax in the fire lighter to make the fire burn longer.

3 Lay a sheet of parchment paper on a level surface and then grip a cotton ball with your tongs or tweezers. Carefully dip it into the wax two or three times and place it on the parchment paper.

4 After a few minutes, when the wax has hardened, wrap your fire lighter with one of the pieces of garden twine two or three times around the wax-coated cotton ball and tie the twine with a double knot. You can also tie on a decorative dried twig or two, or a piece of dried orange peel, if you feel so inclined or if you plan to give a bag of fire lighters as a present. The twine will provide more fibers to carry the flame towards the wax.

5 Use two or three of your fire lighters when lighting a fire, brazier, bonfire, or barbecue, along with dried kindling or tinder and small logs or pieces of coal. Hold the match to the ends of the twine to light your fire lighters.

Hawthorn Gin

Hawthorn is one of the most common shrubs growing in hedgerows and scrubland in temperate areas of Europe, America, and Asia. It's a member of the rose family and, like most varieties of rose hips, hawthorn berries (also known as haws) ripen in September and October. Gathering them in order to make a delicious liqueur as winter gathers pace is no chore. There are often clear, crisp sunny days during autumn, and venturing out to gather haws can make an autumnal walk even lovelier.

This recipe can also be used to make tangy cranberry gin or delicately flavored and deliciously sharp rosehip gin. Wild rose hips from hedgerows are perfect for this. It is best to avoid taking rose hips from neighbors' gardens in case of grumpy recriminations. However, offering a bottle of rose hip gin in return for this harvest seems like an excellent solution.

When the sun goes down and the weather is gruesome, find a cozy spot, light some candles, find a good book (this one would do very well indeed), pour a small glass of one of these fine homemade hedgerow berry-infused liquids and nestle down. There will soon be a glow within and without.

Materials

One 16-ounce (473 ml) canning
  jar with a clamp lid
Sharp scissors
Funnel
One 3-foot (1-m) square of muslin, folded

Ingredients

1½ cups (175 g) hawthorn berries
  (or cranberries)
12 ounces (350 ml) gin
1 cup (200 g) sugar

Makes 2 cups

Note: The seeds inside hawthorn berries can be poisonous, so don't be tempted to sample the berries.

Step by Step

1 Collect enough haw berries to fill the jar in which you plan to make your gin.

2 Wash the berries, and with a pair of sharp scissors, remove any stalks and dried remains of the flower, from the end of each berry. As haws are quite small, this can take some time, so put on a movie or listen to the radio while you work.

3 While you are preparing your haws, you can sterilize your jars. If your jars have rubber seals, remove them. Fill a large pot with enough water to completely submerge your jars. Bring to a boil. Lower your jars and rubber seals into the water. Cover and boil for 10 minutes.

4 Once you've removed the stalks and flower remains, add a layer of haws into your jar around 1½ inches (3 cm) thick. Pour in around a quarter of your sugar.

5 Add another layer of haws, top with sugar, and repeat this process until you have filled the jar. Now pour in your gin.

6 Once you've filled your jar to the top, seal it, and upend it carefully a couple of times in case air has become trapped between the haw berries. Top off with more gin to fill any extra space in the jar.

7 Place your gin on a kitchen shelf or in a cupboard for 4–6 weeks out of direct sunlight. After this time, the color from the berries will have seeped into the gin, resulting in a beautiful pink, rosé wine color.

8 You can let the haws infuse further, but sediment will begin to form at this stage as the berries break down, which can be difficult to remove. To avoid this, sterilize another sealable jar or bottle and place your funnel in the mouth and several layers of muslin into the funnel. Pour your hawthorn gin through the muslin in the funnel and into the second jar or bottle. Discard the berries.

9 Enjoy the gin on its own while nestled under a blanket or with high-quality tonic water.

Hedgerow Bird Snacks

Sitting in a warm room watching birds through a window is immensely relaxing, and knowing that you have put food out to help them survive the coldest weeks of the year makes this even more satisfying. A record of the various species of birds that visit your area is the perfect addition to a regular nature diary and allows you to become familiar with the diversity of birdlife in your local neighbourhood. You may spot winter migrants or more timid species of birds that will emerge to feed when the ground is frosty and most of the wild berries have been eaten.

Many garden centers have a section dedicated to bird food and feeders, but making special snacks for your feathery visitors is not only easy, it also ensures that you know exactly what the birds are eating and can pack their snacks with nutritious ingredients. This recipe includes the hawthorn berries and rose hips that I collect from the bushes in November, but if you make these later in the winter, when fewer wild berries are available, they can be replaced with currants, sultanas, or dried cranberries.

You may need to wait several days or even weeks for your local birds to discover the berry-filled snacks you have made, but as the cold weather begins to bite, food sources like this are essential for survival. They will find your treats eventually.

Materials

1 pound (453 g) lard

4 cups (480 g) total of the following ingredients, in whatever proportion you choose:

Wild berries such as hawthorn or rose hips, or dried fruit

Wild bird seed

Oatmeal

Grated cheese (optional)

Saucepan of boiling water

Heatproof bowl with a diameter larger than that of your saucepan

Coconut halves (available online), small coconut-fiber planters, or yogurt containers

Garden twine

Step by Step

1 Melt your lard by placing a large heatproof bowl over a pan of simmering water.

2 Remove the bowl from the heat and add your berries, dry ingredients, and cheese (if using) to the lard. Blend well with a spoon.

3 Leave the mixture to cool until the lard becomes opaque but is still soft enough to spoon into the coconut halves, the planters, or yogurt containers.

4 Meanwhile, poke a small hole in the bottom of your yogurt containers or coconut-fiber planters with a pencil or small screwdriver (the coconut halves often come with a string already attached).

5 Cut a piece of garden twine around 10 inches (25 cm) long, fold it in half, and tie a double knot to form a loop.

6 Push your loop of string through the hole in the pot so that the knot remains inside.

7 Fill as many of your containers as you can with your mixture and allow it to cool and solidify completely.

8 If you have used yogurt pots, the plastic can be cut away and recycled before you hang your bird snacks outside.

9 Choose a spot in your garden at least 5 feet (1.5 m) off the ground that is tricky for cats and other predators to reach, and with some foliage nearby to shelter shy species of birds between visits to the feeding area.

10 Sit near a window with a warm drink. Watch the birds feeding, record them in your diary, and perhaps even sketch them.

Holidays and Celebrations

Sometimes, the holiday season is so frenetic that the thought of making gifts or accessories by hand seems laughably implausible, and retreating into the closet with a stiff drink for a small cry and a cheering chunk of cake or a large slab of chocolate becomes the far wiser option. On certain days, those closet-hiding, medicinal cake-eating urges must be fulfilled in order to stay sane during the final weeks before you-know-when.

If there were ever a moment to bring a little bit of hygge into your day, it would be during times like these. Hygge celebrates the importance of slowing down and giving yourself permission to take a break. Making a few small gifts in the quiet of a Sunday afternoon allows a check to be added (ever so slightly smugly) to the seemingly endless presents-and-preparation list. An afternoon set aside to crochet a delicate lace necklace or make a wreath to hang on the door will confer a calmness that would hearten anyone in the face of the crazed holiday crescendo. Venturing out to find hazel, willow, ivy, or birch twigs to make into wreaths is an excellent excuse to go for a walk. Trees and green things, even if glimpsed briefly, will help to smooth away the angst of a deadline or a week so full of tasks that you'd like to be a squirrel that knows nothing about shopping lists or budgets.

These projects, particularly suited to pre-shindig preparations but pleasurable to do at any point during winter, are quick to make yet still rather lovely. The making itself is a therapeutic antidote to the seemingly incessant low-level stress that can lurk at this time of year. If you have an hour or two to spare, then the blackberry streusel cake is enough of a delicious showstopper to serve at any get-together, and the slow, steady process of making it while shut away in your kitchen can be a welcome baking escape. Time spent communing with sugar, butter, and ground almonds can be almost as comforting as actually eating them.

Paper Leaf and Berry Bough

The holiday season is the time when I have strong urges to line my house with beautiful handmade things. If I had the time, I would make everything, including hand-crocheted dungarees for the fairy on top of the Christmas tree. In reality, I manage to make two or three items each year—perhaps a decoration and a present or two. Time is tight, to-do lists are long, but crafting is soothing and can help to lower cortisol levels (the stress hormone). Paper crafting is my particular favorite. This design is inspired by mind-bogglingly intricate paper-cut recreations of bucolic winter foliage and dioramas of scampering deer and badgers. I don't have time to spend three days cutting out a perfect paper rendering of an ancient hawthorn bush, so paper punches are an excellent shortcut to conjuring beautiful decorations. These are like hole punches, but with a single hole and used to cut a wide range of shapes out of paper or card stock. This design is inspired by wintry berries and leaves, takes about an hour to make, and is suitable for any winter holiday and beyond.

Materials

2 pieces of letter-sized thin white card stock
Leaf paper punch (the leaf should be
   ¾–1 inch or 2–2.5 cm in length)
Circle paper punch (the circle should be
   ½–¾ inch or 1–2 cm in diameter)
9 inches (22.8 cm) 22-gauge
   silver-plated wire
6 inches (15.2 cm) 18-gauge
   silver-plated wire
Wire cutters
Round-nose pliers
Strong, clear paper glue
Needle nose pliers
Piece of garden twine, around
   10 inches (25 cm) long

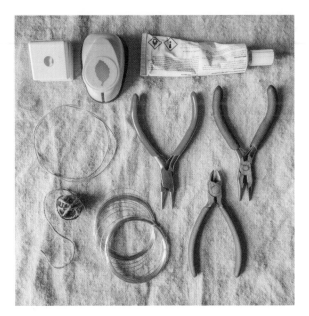

Tip

You can make fewer leaves and berries and twist them together to make smaller, simpler sprigs of foliage. These will be just as attractive but will take less time to make.

Step by Step

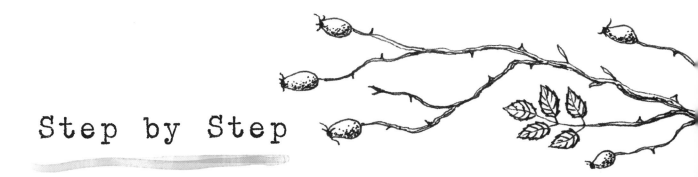

1. Use the leaf paper punch to cut out 36 leaves from the white card stock.

2. Then use the circle paper punch to cut out 30 circles.

3. Use your wire cutters to cut 33 lengths of the 22-gauge wire around 3 inches (8 cm) long and make loops around 1/8 inch (3 mm) in diameter at the end of each one by bending the wire around one of the "noses" of your round-nose pliers.

4. Make each berry by sandwiching a loop of wire between two paper circles with glue. Repeat to make the other 14 berries.

5. Make the 18 leaves in the same way.

6. Bend the 18-gauge silver-plated wire into an arc around 6 inches (15 cm) long and make a loop at each end in the same way as described in step 3.

7. To attach the leaves to the wire, twist the 22-gauge wire extending from a leaf tightly around one end of the arc of the 18-gauge wire so that the 22-gauge wire spirals around it several times. Then trim the excess wire off and squeeze the spiral of 22-gauge wire tightly onto the 18-gauge wire using your needle-nose pliers so that the leaf doesn't slip.

8. Attach 2 more leaves in this way, followed by 3 berries.

9. Repeat this pattern until the whole of the 6-inch (15-cm) arc is filled with leaves and berries and the arc resembles a branch of winter foliage.

10. Tie your garden twine through each loop on the end of your wire arc and hang up your paper bough.

Crochet Lace Necklace

Materials

Rico Essentials Crochet (100% Cotton;
  1.75 ounces/50 g = 284 yards/260 m):
  1 skein in #002 Beige or approximately
  284 yards/260 m of lace weight
  yarn, approximately 2 yards
1.5 mm (size 7) steel crochet hook
Scissors
Yarn needle for weaving in ends
Needle-nose pliers
Wire cutters
2 sterling silver or silver-plated jump
  rings, ¼ inch (6 mm) in diameter
18 inches (45 cm) fine sterling silver
  or silver-plated chain, with links
  around ⅛ inch (3 mm) in diameter

If a party invitation has just dropped into your inbox, or you have a particular friend who deserves a special gift, then this necklace is quick and immensely satisfying. Afterwards you will feel like an accomplished Victorian artisan having conjured what is, in effect, a tiny semicircle of crocheted lace. It sounds complicated and daunting, but it is actually a simple pattern using basic crochet techniques.

At first, it can seem tricky making crochet stitches on such a small scale, but once I had adjusted to the smallness, I found that I reveled in the miniaturization of the familiar patterns of stitches that are usually used to make crochet coasters or mandalas. The slight challenge of the scale is countered by the speed with which these necklaces can be made. I am far from nimble when crocheting with such a tiny hook (as I'm overdue a visit to the optician), but it takes me only around twenty minutes to make the crochet part of this design. A whole afternoon sitting in front of *It's a Wonderful Life* and you could go into production and have a stall at your local craft fair.

Abbreviations & Definitions

ch chain
sk skip
sp space
sl st slip stitch
sc single crochet
dc double crochet
tr treble crochet
yo yarn over
st/s stitch/es
hdc half double crochet: yo, insert hook, yo, pull through, yo, pull through all 3 loops on hook

Pattern

To begin, make a slip knot and ch 6,
joining with a sl st to form a ring.

Row 1: ch 1 (does not count as st throughout),
10 sc into the ch ring. Turn.
Make sure you make your stitches close to
one another so that they form a semicircle
rather than fill the whole ring.
Row 2: ch 6 (counts as 1 dc and 3 ch sp), sk 1 sc at
base of chain, dc 1 into next sc, *ch 3, sk 1 sc, dc 1
into next sc; repeat from * 3 more times. Turn.
Row 3: ch 1, sk 1 dc, sc 5 into 3 ch sp, ch 1,
*sc 5 into next 3 ch sp, ch 1; repeat from * 2
more times, sc 5 into final 3 ch sp. Turn.
Row 4: ch 1, sc 1, ch 4, sk 4 sc, sc 1 into 1 ch sp,
*ch 4, sk 5 sc, sc 1 into 1 ch sp; repeat from * 2
more times, ch 4, sk 4 sc, sc 1 into last sc. Turn.
Row 5: *ch 1, sk 1 sc, [sc 1, hdc 2, dc 1, hdc 2, sc 1]
into 4 ch sp; repeat from * 4 more times.
Fasten off and weave in ends.

Step by Step

1 Iron your crochet semicircle on a setting
suitable for your yarn.

2 Close your chain at the clasp, find the center of
the chain, and use your wire cutters to cut the
chain in half.

3 Use your pliers to open one of the jump rings
slightly. Thread the end of it through into
the top right-hand corner of the crochet lace
semicircle you have made, holding the semicircle
so that the curved edge is pointing downward.
Thread the same jump ring through one of the
links on the end of your chain. Close the jump
ring using your pliers.

4 Repeat step 3 with the second jump ring,
attaching it to the other corner of your crochet
lace semicircle.

5 Try on the necklace and admire your exquisite
handiwork.

If you're a beginner
and would like to
learn the basic crochet
stitches, you can find
full instructions on my
website: silverpebble.net.

Blackberry and Almond Streusel Cake

It's December. Friends are coming over and dessert is required. Cocooning yourself in your kitchen for a baking session may sound like hard work, but the making of this cake is gently reassuring, and at the end of it, you'll be rewarded with something irresistible, combining moist, rich cake filled with fruit and an indulgent buttery crumble-like topping.

The hedges are blackberry-free zones during winter, but if you froze some earlier in the year or can find some frozen ones from your local grocer or in a supermarket freezer, then they don't even have to be defrosted. In fact, adding the frozen berries directly to the cake mix before you put it in the oven means that they just soften and poach gently while the cake bakes, leaving them with just the right amount of bite when the cake is done.

This cake does have a special occasion sort of feel to it. The trickiest part of this recipe may be resisting eating a chunk of it before your visitors arrive.

Ingredients

For the cake:
⅔ cup (80 g) self-rising flour
⅔ cup (80 g) ground almonds
⅓ cup (40 g) cornmeal
Zest of 1 lemon
1 teaspoon baking powder
1 cup (200g) superfine sugar
14 tablespoons (200 g) butter, softened
3 large eggs
2 cups (283 g) frozen blackberries, plums, or raspberries

For the streusel topping:
4 tablespoons (57 g) butter, cold
⅔ cup (80 g) all-purpose flour
¼ cup (50 g) demerara sugar
⅓ cup (45 g) pine nuts

Serves 8–10

Step by Step

1 Set your oven to 350°F (180°C).

2 Line a 9-inch (23-cm) springform pan with parchment paper. I don't worry about origami—I just push a big 16-inch (40-cm) square of it into the tin. When it's baked, it looks like a large muffin.

3 First, make the streusel topping by rubbing the 4 tablespoons butter into the flour and demerara sugar using your fingertips. When it looks like rough bread crumbs, add the pine nuts, mix to distribute them, and set aside.

4 Combine the flour, almonds, cornmeal, and baking powder into another bowl along with the lemon zest. Set aside.

5 In a separate bowl, cream the softened butter and superfine sugar with an electric mixer until it's pale and fluffy.

6 Add one of the eggs and whisk to blend.

7 Add about a third of the flour mixture. Fold in thoroughly with a large spoon.

8 Repeat steps 6 and 7 twice more until no more eggs or flour mixture are left.

9 Fold your blackberries (or plums or raspberries) into the cake mix. They will tend to clump, as they are frozen, so try to distribute them evenly throughout.

10 Pour the mixture into your lined pan, spread it to the sides, and smooth the surface with a knife.

11 Wipe any splatters of cake batter away from the edge of the parchment paper with some paper towel. If you leave them, they will burn.

12 Sprinkle the streusel topping on the top of the batter.

13 Bake for 40–50 minutes. Check the cake after 25 minutes—if it's getting quite brown, cover it with foil and remove it from the oven after it's been baking for 40 minutes.

14 After 40 minutes, insert a toothpick and check if it comes out clean. If the cake is also coming away from the edges of the tin a tiny bit and springs back when you poke it with your finger, it should be done. Put it back in the oven for another 5–10 minutes if it does not spring back.

15 Allow the cake to cool a little on a rack. Eat with large dollops of whipped cream.

The Berry Cocktail

Sometimes, a little bit of booze is needed. And sometimes, it needs to be sweet and prettily colored and sipped while watching an old film on a chilly evening beneath a soft blanket. This recipe hits that spot. It's easy to make and perfect for drinking by the fire. You can use a nip of the hawthorn gin (page 50) or a simple, delicious blackberry syrup that, with some brief simmering, distills the flavor of late summer so that you can taste it in your glass. All poetic thoughts aside, it will cheer you right up if there's a storm blowing outside, you dropped your bag in a puddle, or you've yet to shovel your driveway. It is reassuring and very lovely.

Ingredients

For the cocktail:

1 ounce (30 ml) sloe, damson, hawthorn
   or rosehip gin (see page 50 for recipe) or
   blackberry syrup (recipe on next page)
2 ounces (60 ml) your favorite white wine
2 ounces (60 ml) tonic water
A few fresh berries (optional)

For the blackberry syrup:

2¼ cups (350 g) frozen blackberries
1 cup (200 g) sugar
Splash of water

Makes 1 drink

Rubus fruticosus

Step by Step

Blackberry Syrup

1 To make a simple blackberry syrup, simmer the frozen blackberries with a good splash of water and the sugar until the fruit just breaks down and the juice is released. Don't allow it to thicken.

2 Strain the syrup through a sieve into a sterilized bottle and keep it in the fridge—you can save the pulp and eat it with your breakfast cereal.

Cocktail

1 Combine all the cocktail ingredients in a glass. Add the blackberry syrup to taste.

2 Add a few fresh berries to your glass for decoration, if you like.

3 Curl up and toast the summer that was.

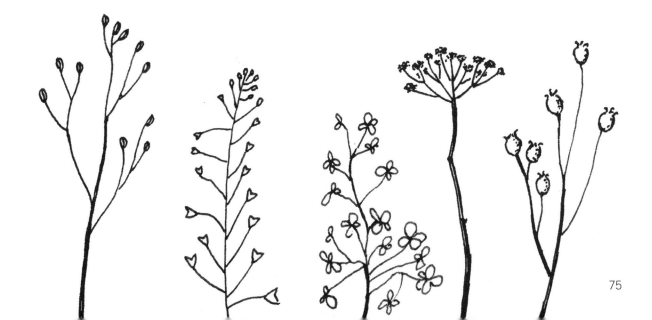

Woodland Wreaths

When the calendar moves beyond the beginning of December, many people hang a wreath on their door. You can, of course, buy premade wreaths, usually constructed from Christmas tree branches. Artificial ones are pretty common, too. While these store-bought ones are festive, making your own wreath from branches and twigs you found on a walk is thrifty and satisfying and will help to boost your feel-good neurotransmitters by getting you outside and channeling your creativity. The wreaths you make will be natural, charming, and often more delicate. You're also likely to be reluctant to put them away in the New Year. Wreaths made from foraged twigs are beautiful enough to be hung on doors and walls all year round.

The simplest wreaths of all—and perhaps the most elegant —consist of a single branch, stem, or bundle of fine stems bent carefully into a circle and fixed in place with galvanized wire or garden twine. A collection of such smallish, delicate wreaths made this way and hung on a wall bring a lovely festive feel to a room and are easy on the pocket.

Materials

Pruning shears
Plant material collected from your
  garden, local park, or countryside*
Wire cutters
14-gauge galvanized steel wire,
  garden twine, or raffia

*If you'd like to cut material from someone's garden, then do ask permission. Similarly, ask permission if you'd like to take plant material from parks. In the countryside, removing a few stems of ivy or a branch or two of beech will not do harm, but do not take too much as it may weaken the plant.

Woodland Plants and Shrubs to Look Out For

Willow

Willow (*Salix*) likes to grow with its roots in moist ground. It often grows along rivers or canals or on the edges of ponds or lakes. Its stems and branches are straight yet very flexible, and it has been used as a material for basket-, fence- and garden structures in many countries for millennia. Willow makes smooth, uniform wreaths, which can be used as an excellent base for adding other plants, such as ivy, wild clematis, or beech leaves (you can preserve the leaves in autumn so you have them on hand for winter—see page 15). The flowers of pussy or goat willow are furry, gray, and very soft. Wreaths made with these varieties are a gorgeous way to celebrate the approach of spring.

Herbs

Woody herbs such as rosemary and certain varieties of thyme can be used to make tiny wreaths as their stems are sturdy yet flexible. They work well as pleasantly scented, natural decorations for simply wrapped gifts, for table settings, or for hanging on your tree.

Beech

Beech (*Fagus*) is one of my favorite trees. Its bark is smooth and almost silvery gray; its new spring foliage is that joyous bright acid green that announces spring's arrival; and they turn the most beautiful copper color in autumn. This tree's bare wintry branches with their regularly spaced buds form such beautiful patterns against the sky that whenever I see this sight I find myself reaching for pen and paper. The slender twigs and branches are flexible, and a wreath made from just one or two of them is simple, elegant, and perfectly wintry.

Birch

Birch (*Betula*) is a pioneer species. When new land forms in a sand dune or on the edge of a fen, it is one of the first trees to grow. Its branches end in bundles of fine, very flexible woody stems that make simple, attractive wreaths. They carry small catkin-like flowers during autumn and into winter, which add texture to birch wreaths and make them a great subject for simple botanical drawings.

Ivy

This is a common wild plant species around the world and was introduced to the United States by English colonists in 1727. Its young stems, which can be up to five feet (1.5 m) long, cannot support themselves so the plant tends to cling to walls or the trunks of trees. Like species of clematis, its habit of climbing means that its stems must be flexible, making it a perfect plant to use for wreaths.

Hazel

Varieties of hazel tree (*Corylus*) are present on most continents, and the branches of this tree have been used to weave fences and gates since farming began. The wood of the hazel is not quite as flexible as willow, nor as straight, but the wreaths it makes are simple and beautiful. This tree has the added bonus of bearing delicious nuts in autumn and catkins (male flowers) from November onwards. The young catkins add lovely detail to wreaths made using hazel.

Wild and Garden Varieties of Clematis

Clematis vitalba or "Traveler's Joy" grows wild in the United Kingdom, Europe, Australia and the United States and is so called because its delicate silvery flower heads cover the hedgerows in winter, making them gleam rather wonderfully in low light and offering walkers a welcome spectacle. Each seed head consists of soft, whitish hair-like fibers that resemble hairs, giving rise to its other colloquial name "Old man's beard." *Clematis ternifolia* is a wild Japanese relative of *vitalba* with similar delicate, fuzzy flower heads.

Most clematis varieties, including both wild and domesticated species, have a climbing, twining habit, and so their stems are naturally flexible. This makes them excellent candidates for making free-form delicate wreaths.

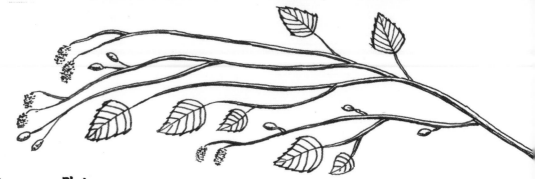

Step by Step

1. To make a large wreath to hang on your front door or above the fireplace, choose at least two twigs or stems, around 15–25 inches (40–60 cm) long. If you're using birch, find two bundles of flexible branches about this length.

2. Cut several lengths of galvanized wire or garden twine, around 8 inches (20 cm) long.

3. If your twigs or stems are from hazel or willow trees then bend them over your knee once or twice before you begin to encourage them to curve.

4. Lay the thick end of one of your twigs or stems so that it overlaps by several inches with the thin end of another. Bind the two together with wire or twine. If you're using galvanized wire, wind it four or five times around both twigs as tightly as you can.

5. Bring the other ends of your stems or twigs together and bind again.

6. You may need to tie the twigs together at a few more points around your wreath to ensure it is sturdy and forms a rough circular shape.

7. Hang on a door, a wall, or with other wreaths to make a gorgeous display.

The Grayest Days

The recent sleet has turned the garden into a muddy wasteland, and stepping outside is like an icy assault on your face and mood. There's no snow to perk up the look of your crispy perennials, your cat has become a morose recluse, and your toes feel as cold as granite. It is in times like these when emergency plans are needed. A walk would require emerging from the comfort of your house and being bombarded by spiky rain or mushy snowflakes, so hibernation, contingency plans, and mood-boosting comfort foods are required. What could be more hygge than a day indulging in these simple pleasures?

I find it a reassuring thought that just a few minutes after emerging from a nest of quilts and blankets, you could be creeping back beneath them armed with a mug of chocolatey, saucy cake and a spoon. My chocolate cake in a mug is not only delicious, but the antioxidant trans-resveratrol found in the cocoa has been shown to boost serotonin levels. In effect, this compound acts as a natural antidepressant: chocolate really can cheer you up, so a lightning quick, cocoa-rich mug cake is the perfect antidote to freezing temperatures and slate gray skies.

Gentle, meditative craft can help distract the mind from the damp horror of the weather. The hawthorn wrist warmers (page 88) are covered in little three dimensional crocheted berries and stems. Watching tiny sprigs of hawthorn manifest as you make the stitches is a lovely process, and you'll be left with mitts that not only channel classic botanical designs, but will also keep your hands snug on a winter walk (when the weather starts to perk up a bit). Assembling delicate, beaded garland necklaces with subtly twinkly gemstones or spending some time making simple, botanical-inspired watercolor drawings are projects that perfectly suit a slow indoor winter day.

Five-Minute Molten Chocolate Cake in a Mug

I'm sure you remember the feeling, or perhaps you're experiencing it now: winter has worn away your energy and all you want to do is snooze. You're craving something delicious, but the thought of measuring and mixing and then waiting for a cake to bake seems just too much. Enter this utterly brilliant recipe.

Gooey, satisfying chocolate cake in a mug seems almost too miraculous to be true, but I can confirm that this holy grail of chocolate sauce–filled instant cakes tastes like those fancy desserts you might be served in a restaurant. Plus, it is made from pantry ingredients in five minutes (thanks to the wonders of the microwave). On a particularly grim wintry day, omit the salted caramel sauce for speed, although the combination of salt-tinged liquid toffee with the rich dark chocolate cake and sauce is a taste like no other. Follow with a nap among quilts and blankets, and that bleak Sunday afternoon suddenly seems a good deal more appealing.

Ingredients

For the cake:
3 tablespoons all-purpose flour
  (gluten-free flour also works fine)
2 tablespoons high-quality cocoa powder
¼ teaspoon baking powder
2 tablespoons superfine sugar
  (1½ tablespoons for a slightly more
  grown-up, less sweet version)
Pinch of salt
2 tablespoons vegetable oil
6 tablespoons milk

For the salted caramel sauce:
⅓ cup (75 g) light brown sugar
6 tablespoons (150 g) heavy cream
2 tablespoons (25 g) butter
Pinch of salt

Makes 2 small cakes

Step by Step

1 If you're planning on making the salted caramel, place all the ingredients for the sauce into a saucepan on low heat and stir until the sugar dissolves. Then allow to bubble for 3–4 minutes until the sauce thickens. Set to one side, while you move on to the cake.

2 Place all the dry ingredients into a jug or bowl with a pouring spout and make a well in the center.

3 Beat continually with a whisk or fork as you slowly add the oil to the well. Then begin to add the milk in the same way.

4 Continue to whisk steadily to get rid of any clumps of flour. The mixture should become glossy and thick.

5 Divide the mixture between two microwave-safe mugs.

6 Drop a tablespoon or so of your salted caramel mixture (if you have made it) into the center of the cake batter in your mug.

7 Microwave each mug individually on full power (750 or 800 W) for 40 seconds. This leaves a puddle of hot, still-molten chocolate and salted caramel sauce in the center of the dessert. This will solidify to a delicious chocolate and toffee-like, fudgey substance as it cools.

8 If you prefer a solid chocolate and salted caramel cake, then microwave for 50–60 seconds. It will be volcanically hot, so allow it to cool for a minute or two.

9 Pour cream or spoon a dollop of crème fraîche on top. Eat with glee.

Hawthorn Wrist Warmers

If the outside world really seems just too dreary and gray to face, then staying indoors and conjuring some berries with a crochet hook and yarn comes a close second to seeing the real things growing in a hedge. This pattern is a challenge, but once you have established the central and right-hand stems, there is a rhythm to the pattern that is engrossing and pleasing as the branches and berries appear. Also, as it's a pattern that needs a good deal of concentration it is particularly good diversion from daily stresses.

I used two skeins of DK Eden Cottage Yarns Bowland in Misty Woods for my wrist warmers. It's the color of lichen, soothing to the eye and super soft. Beautiful artisanal yarn like this increases the aesthetic joy of making an item by hand. Once your wrist warmers are finished, not only will your hands be exquisitely swaddled, but you may just find yourself finally equipped to face the outdoors. Of course, whether you choose to venture past your threshold or simply sit back and admire your new mittens wrapped around a mug of something steaming is another matter.

Materials

Eden Cottage Yarns Bowland
   (100% Superwash Bluefaced Leicester;
   3.5 ounces/
   100 g = 245 yards/224 m): 2 skeins
   in Misty Woods or approximately 490
   yards/448 m of DK weight yarn (3)
4 mm (size G-6) crochet hook
Scissors
Yarn needle for weaving in ends

Abbreviations & Definitions

ch chain
sk skip
sl st slip stitch
sc single crochet
dc double crochet
tr treble crochet
yo yarn over
st/s stitch/es
tog together
tr treble: yo twice, insert hook, yo, pull
   through, [yo, pull through 2 loops] 3 times
inc increase: work 2 dc in 1 stitch
FPtr front post treble: yo twice, then
   instead of inserting hook into the top of
   the next stitch, poke it behind and then in
   front of the post of the next stitch 2 rows
   below and pull up a loop (4 loops on hook)
   then (yo pull through 2 loops) 3 times to
   complete the stitch. This creates a raised
   treble stitch and resembles a cable stitch.
berry dc4tog: * yo, insert hook into
   stitch, yo, pull through, yo, pull through
   two loops; rep from * three more times;
   yo pull through all 5 loops on hook

Round 13: Repeat Round 1.

Rounds 14-21: Repeat Rounds 6-13.

Round 22 (increase round): ch 3, dc 5, inc in next st, dc 4, inc in next st, dc 2, work berry in next st, dc 1, RLS (part 2), work berry in next st, dc 1, CS, [dc 4, inc in next st] 3 times, dc 5, join with a sl st (45 sts).

Round 23: Repeat Round 1.

Round 24: ch 3, dc 17, work berry in next st, dc 2, CS, dc 1, LLS (part 1), dc 21, join with a sl st.

Round 25: Repeat Round 1.

Round 26: ch 3, dc 20, CS, dc 1, work berry in next st, LLS (part 2), dc 1, work berry in next st, dc 18, join with a sl st.

Round 27 (thumb gap round): ch 1, sc in each st to last 13 sts, ch 7 loosely, sk next 12 sts, sc 1, join with a sl st .

Round 28: ch 3, dc 18, RLS (part 1), dc 1, CS, dc 2, work berry in next st, dc in each st to end (working 7 dc across 7 ch of previous row), join with a sl st (40 sts).

Round 29: Repeat Round 1.

Round 30: ch 3, dc 15, work berry in next st, dc 1, RLS (part 2), work berry in next st, dc 1, CS, dc 18, join with a sl st.

Round 31: Repeat Round 1.

Round 32: ch 3, dc 17, work berry in next st, dc4, LLS (part 1), dc 16, join with a sl st.

Round 33: Repeat Round 1.

Round 34: ch 3, dc 22, work berry in next st, LLS (part 2), dc 1, work berry in next st, dc 13, join with a sl st.

Round 35: Repeat Round 1.

Round 36: ch 3, dc 23, work berry in next st, dc 15, join with a sl st.

Round 37: Repeat Round 1.

Round 38: Repeat Round 2.

Round 39: Repeat Round 1.

Fasten off and weave in ends.

Left-Hand Wrist Warmer

To begin, work a loose foundation chain of 40 stitches. Join your chain with a sl st to work in the round, being careful not to twist the chain.

Rounds 1–26: Work Rounds 1–26 from the RH wrist warmer pattern.

Round 27 (thumb gap round): ch 1, sc 1, ch 7 loosely, sk next 12 sts, sc in next st and each st to end, join with a sl st.

Round 28: ch 3, dc 13, (working 7 dc across 7 ch of previous row), RLS (part 1), dc 1, CS, dc 2, work berry in next st, dc 20, join with a sl st (40 sts).

Round 29: Repeat Round 1.

Round 30: ch 3, dc 10, work berry in next st, dc 1, RLS (part 2), work berry in next st, dc 1, CS, dc 23, join with a sl st.

Round 31: Repeat Round 1.

Round 32: ch 3, dc 12, work berry in next st, dc 4, LLS (part 1), dc 21, join with a sl st.

Round 33: Repeat Round 1.

Round 34: ch 3, dc 17, work berry in next st, LLS (part 2), dc 1, work berry in next st, dc 18, join with a sl st.

Round 35: Repeat Round 1.

Round 36: ch 3, dc 18, work berry in next st, dc 20, join with a sl st.

Round 37: Repeat Round 1.

Round 38: Repeat Round 2.

Round 39: Repeat Round 1.

Fasten off and weave in ends.

If you're a beginner and would like to learn the basic crochet stitches, you can find full instructions on my website: silverpebble.net.

Beaded Garland Necklace

You may have noticed that I rather like plants. I draw them, press them into silver clay, record the progression of flowering species in the hedgerows near our cottage, and even fashion them out of paper. If I could make a hat out of pussy willow or cow parsley and wear it to the supermarket without being laughed at, I would.

I've been making and selling jewelery since 1997, and one of the first necklaces I made was a tiny garland of gemstone beads hanging from a delicate chain. The beads were equally spaced, and as I added each one, the design began to remind me of tiny berries along a stem. I went on to make many of these simple garland necklaces and sold them at craft fairs and online.

Learning to attach a bead to a chain doesn't take long, and once the steps are mastered, there are innumerable combinations of freshwater pearls, gemstones, and glass or metal beads that can be used to make a range of necklaces (and bracelets if you choose a shorter chain) that any pirate would covet. Attaching just five tiny freshwater pearls or faceted garnets in the center of a delicate chain will make a truly beautiful necklace. If I were given one as a gift, I'd be over the moon.

Materials

Needle-nose pliers
Round-nose pliers
Wire cutters
Delicate silver-plated or sterling
   silver chain with links around
   1/8 inch (3 mm) in diameter
Silver-plated or sterling sterling silver
   1-inch or 1½-inch head pins, 26-gauge*
Your choice of beads (gemstones,
   freshwater pearls, silver, or glass)

*Note: The holes drilled through most gemstone beads are around 0.5 mm wide. If you buy ball pins that are larger than 26-gauge, they may be too thick to thread through your beads.

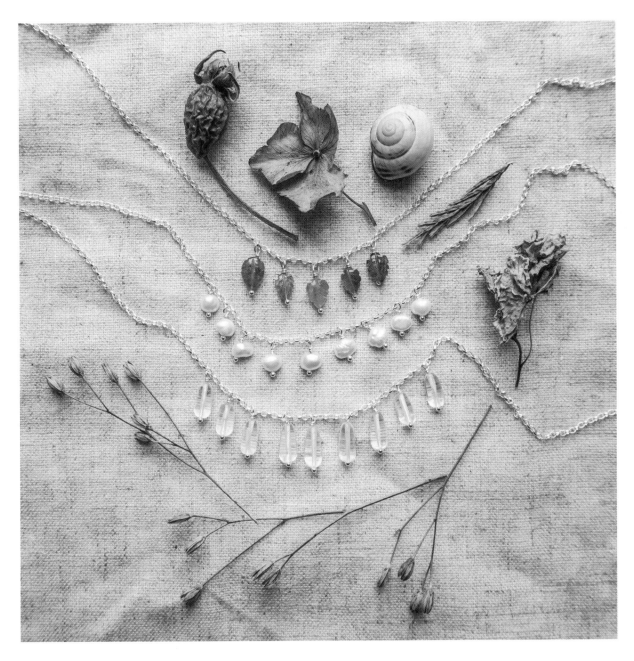

Step by Step

1 Find the center of your chain by closing the clasp and then holding it at the clasp and allowing the chain to fall free. Then pinch the chain in the middle. You can mark that central link with a little loop of wire or cotton thread to aid the later steps.

2 Thread each of your beads onto its own head pin.

3 Grasp a ball head pin with a bead threaded onto it with your round-nose pliers, about ⅛ inch (3 mm) above the top of bead.

4 Hold your round-nose pliers so you are looking down their "noses."

5 Push the bead and the part of the head pin inserted into the bead to the left slightly. If the tip of your pliers were the center of a clock face, you would move the bead and the wire to the 7 o'clock position.

6 Push the wire end of the head pin tightly around the right-hand "nose" of the pliers so that it passes in front of the bead. You are essentially locking the bead in place and creating a loop of wire just above it.

7 Take the looped head pin and bead off the pliers. Hook the wire end of the head pin through the central link of your chain. Pull the wire so that the loop you have made is sitting in that link.

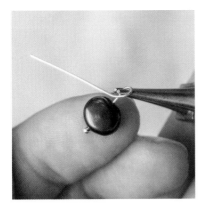  

8 Using your needle-nose pliers, grip the wire loop you have made across its center, ensuring the chain drapes freely behind the loop.

9 Using your fingers, twist the wire end of the head pin around the central wire of the head pin to form a tight spiral. Continue making the spiral until the wire just touches the top of the bead.

10 Use your wire cutters to snip the excess wire at the end of the head pin away from the bead.

11 Use your needle-nose pliers to pinch the end of the wire you've just cut so that it won't scratch your skin when you wear the necklace.

12 Repeat steps 3–11 for the next bead, inserting it a few links away from your central bead.

13 If you'd like your garland necklace to resemble berries or buds on a stem, then keep the spacing between your beads consistent by counting the links before you add each bead. Alternatively, you can randomly space your beads.

14 If you're making the necklace for yourself, then trying it on and admiring it in the mirror is a critical final step.

Watercolor Botanical Motifs

When I was quite small I had a watercolor set, and until I was about thirteen, I painted fairly regularly—simple landscapes, patterns, and studies of birds from photographs in books. As I began to study for my school exams, art disappeared from my class schedule, and it seems that I stopped painting at home, too. I have no paintings made during my teens. I revived my watercolor painting for a brief period in college, but other than that, I had hardly picked up a paintbrush until last year. When I did, I remembered the sensation of being entirely immersed in the mixing of colors and the making of marks on paper.

It has been shown that when mammals make repetitive movements their serotonin levels increase.[1] It is likely that this applies to humans and may explain some human behaviors, such as parents rocking their children to sleep. Small tracking movements made by the eyes and the hands during creative activities seem to have beneficial and soothing psychological effects and may also be linked to the release of feel-good neurotransmitters. One creative way of triggering this soothing effect is by painting. There is a repetitiveness to the actions required while painting with watercolors in particular—you dip a paintbrush into water, brush it onto the paint, touch the brush on to the palette to deposit the paint, rinse the brush, repeat, and mix the paint in the palette until the desired color is created. Making paint marks on paper also requires the hands and eyes to move gently backwards and forwards as the paint is transferred from the brush to the paper's surface.

As with drawing, it is easy to feel that the paintings we may make won't be worth seeing, that there's no value in even beginning because they will never end up in a gallery. But that's missing the point. The ability to be creative was crucial to our survival as hunter-gatherers and as Stone Age and Bronze Age humans. It was selected for over many generations. Communicating with other human beings, and making marks on rocks, or the walls of caves, and in the soil or sand were essential for our ancestors. Picking up a brush, mixing a paint color, and using that brush to make even the simplest marks on paper taps into something ancient. That something may have become very quiet over the course of many generations but can be awoken. The process of making brushstrokes can help drown out life's noisy treadmill and dial down stress levels. The feeling is similar to that experienced during meditation or yoga.

1 Rows or clusters of brush marks or very simple shapes are a great place to start with watercolurs. Choose a single color and its intensity as you make more marks. Think of the color gradation in a rainbow or color wheel, choose your favorite two or three colors, and remix your paint color every few strokes so that your watercolor pattern develops a pleasing subtle ombre appearance.

2 Next, make a fine line or two in whatever color you choose. Using a different color, add a very simple circular or leaf shape. Several of these super simple sprigs make a very satisfying and attractive pattern. Alternatively, you can embellish them a little more.

3 From a point a third of the way along the line from the circular or leaf-shaped mark you have made, make several more lines towards that end point. Add the same simple leaf or round berry-like shape to the end of those lines, too. You can create rose hips or hawthorn berries, winter seed heads, and clusters of leaves.

4 Another way to make a simple and beautiful botanical motif is to simply add more leaf or berry shapes on either side of the single stem you have painted. This will resemble winter buds, beech nuts, or evergreen species such as cotoneaster.

1. Research by Dr. Barry Jacobs of Princeton University has found that repetitive movements in mammals, such as the licking of fur, enhance the release of serotonin, associated with lifted mood. http://www.sciencedirect.com/science/article/pii/1044576595900047

Looking Ahead to Spring

Until recent years, I viewed the seasons as discrete collections of months, each inducing distinct feelings—spring with hope, summer with contentment, autumn with trepidation, and winter with gloom. To my shame, I have rarely gardened during the winter months and the perennials from any particular summer are often still there when spring arrives, in desperate need of pruning shears and a bonfire, all dried out and forlorn. I used to connect gardening and nature with warmer, sunnier months, neglecting my trowel entirely when the leaves started dropping, and barely glanced at the hedges or woods because they were not filled with primroses, cow parsley, or cherry blossoms. I realize that this was foolhardy. The seasons are not separate like the rooms of a house. They blend subtly into one another and sometimes there are encouraging signs of an approaching season to be found six months or more before it arrives. I began to realize that planning spring and summer activities in the midst of the colder weather can be very heartening. Seed catalogs are things of beauty and filled with color: marigolds, tomatoes, cornflowers, and kale. Shopping for seeds is (almost) guilt-free: bulbs cost less than a fancy dress and planting them in pots indoors will ensure that you bring spring forward and have a gorgeous floral display for the New Year.

Overlooking the tiny catkins and tentative baby shoots outside was foolish, but what I also didn't realize was that digging itself can be beneficial. The gentle exercise of pushing a spade or trowel into soil and the sunlight in the garden will boost serotonin, which will lift your mood. Recent research is beginning to show that exposure to soil bacteria can also raise the levels of this mood-boosting neurotransmitter. If you can face the chilly temperatures, then contact with the soil itself can be an antidote to the grayest of days: getting muddy (and admittedly a bit cold) among the winter flower beds is a good thing.

New Year Bulbs

There's a period of two months or so between the weeks leading up to the holiday season and the earliest signs of spring's arrival in February, when color is at its most scarce in the countryside. Most of the berries have been eaten by birds, the previous year's flowers and autumn leaves have died away, and the earliest blossoms and blooms have yet to emerge. It's dreary. There are some winter-flowering plants that can provide spots of color, but most of these are found in domestic gardens rather than on a winter walk.

There is a way to bring the subtle color of late February and March forward into late December and New Year though. If bulbs are planted indoors in September and October and kept relatively cool and dark, they will grow more quickly than their cousins outdoors. It is possible to have the cheery yellow of narcissi, the subtle blue of grape hyacinths, and the simple white bells of snowdrops flowering indoors in January and, in some cases, late December—it's your very own early spring.

Materials

Spring bulbs from a garden store
Containers—anything from enamel
    bowls to jam jars or small
    galvanized buckets will do
All-purpose compost
Pea gravel or pieces of broken clay flowerpot
Black garbage bag, hessian
    sacking, or old fabric
Twigs and twine to support the stems

Note: You will also need a cool, dark place to store your bulb containers, such as a shed, garage, or unheated room.

Choose Your Bulbs

Europe and North America:
Crocus, hyacinth, daffodil/narcissus (e.g. miniature varieties such as Tete-a-Tete and taller early varieties such as paperwhite), miniature iris (e.g. *Iris reticulata*), grape hyacinth (*Muscari*), Siberian squill (*Scilla siberica*).

Asia:
Crocus, narcissus, starflower, hyacinth.

Australia:
Narcissus, starflower, grape hyacinth, Ixia.

Snowdrops:
Snowdrops are native to Europe but can be commonly found on sale in garden stores around the world. They can be forced using this method, but it is best to make a note of where clumps of snowdrops may have already naturalized in your garden and transplant a small clump of them into a container indoors in the autumn. Store-bought bulbs that are planted inside take several years to establish and spread. Alternatively, perhaps you could swap a tray of plum blondies or a blackberry streusel cake (page 22 and page 68) for a clump of snowdrop bulbs from a neighbor's garden.

Choose Your Container

Choose the containers you will use for forcing your bulbs. Jam jars work well, and seeing the roots through the glass is a great way to teach children about how plants grow and absorb water. Old clay plant pots always look beautiful, especially if they are aged and have patches of moss or lichen growing on them. Simple white enamel bowls, dishes, or mugs are good too, although they don't have drainage holes. To prevent water from pooling at the base of any enamel vessels you're using or other containers that do not have drainage holes, place a handful of pea gravel or some broken pieces of clay pot at the bottom of your enamelware.

Step by Step

1 Place a layer of compost on the bottom of your container (on top of the gravel or pieces of clay pot, if you are using them). Fill the container until it comes up to around 1½ inches (4 cm) from the rim for larger bulbs such as narcissi or hyacinths, and 1 inch (2–3 cm) for smaller bulbs such as snowdrops, crocuses, or squill.

2 Place your bulbs on top of this lower layer of compost. You can plant them fairly close together to create a dense display of flowers, but try not to allow them to touch each other, as this might cause them to rot.

3 Cover the bulbs with more compost so that just the tips of them protrude above the surface. Once the shoots emerge, it is sometimes tricky to distinguish one variety of bulb from another, so label them at this stage.

4 Put your containers onto a plastic or metal tray or onto individual saucers. Water them so that the soil becomes moist but not sodden.

5 Place your containers of bulbs in a cold but dryish place, such as a shed, the corner of a garage, or a cool cupboard that is not near a radiator. Cover the pots with an unsealed black garbage bag, hessian sack, or 2–3 layers of old fabric so that the light is blocked out.

6 Check your bulbs every 2 weeks or so. If the compost has become dry, then water it a little. Once the shoots have reached 1–2 inches

(3–5 cm) tall you can move your containers onto a light, cool windowsill. For most bulbs, this will require 8–10 weeks or so in their cool, dark spot. Paperwhite narcissi will grow more quickly and may only need 5–7 weeks.

7 Once your bulbs have been brought out into the light, avoid placing them in a very warm or dry spot, as they will need to acclimatize to the new warmer, lighter conditions. They will, however, need light to allow their shoots to develop further; 6–8 hours a day is ideal at this stage, but you don't need to worry too much.

8 At this point, the bulbs may grow rather quickly and become leggy. To avoid this, ensure they are near a window, but if it occurs, simply stake your plants with twigs and twine or gently wrap the twine two to three times around the cluster of leaves and tie them together to provide a little support.

9 Place your containers of bulbs where they'll cheer you up most—next to your bed or near the front door so you encounter them as you come home.

Hellebore Boot Cuffs

One of the earliest and most beautiful flowers to come into bud in late winter here in the Fens is the hellebore. The sight is as joyous to me as a glimpse of the first swallow in April. The oriental varieties are deeply colored, rather elegant, and their shape is the classic five-petaled flower on a tallish stalk that I used to draw as a little girl. Unlike more subtle late-winter flowers such as snowdrops or aconites, hellebores are unmissable. They seem to shout the approach of spring just when you've been florally deprived for three months and need them the most. I love them for that.

These boot cuffs will make your legs cozy on winter walks and will turn your rain boots from functional footwear into something rather eye-catching. In order to closely match the colors of hellebore petals, I've used chunky Malabrigo Mecha yarn in Lotus, but any soft chunky yarn whose color cheers you up would do.

Materials

Malabrigo Mecha (100% Superwash Merino Wool; 3.5 ounces/100 g = 142 yards/130 m): 2 skeins in #120 Lotus or approximately 284 yards/260 m of chunky weight yarn (5)
6 mm (size J-10) crochet hook
Scissors
Yarn needle for weaving in ends

Abbreviations & Definitions

ch chain
sk skip
sl st slip stitch
sc single crochet
.dc double crochet
tr treble crochet
yo yarn over
st/s stitch/es
tog together
2 trtog treble 2 sts together: yo twice, insert hook into specified st, yo, pull through, [yo, pull through 2 loops] twice; yo twice, insert hook into specified st, yo, pull through, [yo, pull through 2 loops] twice* yo and pull through all 3 loops on hook; when working more tr together, work as above repeating between * and * as many times as necessary, then yo and pull through all remaining loops on hook
petal 3 trtog or [3 ch, 2 trtog] forming a petal of the hellebore motif; both of these stitch combinations are used to form petal motifs in this pattern

Stretch Rib Section (Worked Flat)

To begin, work a loose foundation chain of 11 stitches.

Row 1: sk 1st ch, sc in each ch to end. Turn.
Row 2: ch 1 (does not count as st throughout), sc in back loop only in each sc to end. Turn.
Rows 3–48: Repeat Row 2. For smaller-sized cuffs, repeat 38 more times for a total of 40 rows instead.
To finish: sl st ends of work together to form a tube.

Hellebore Cuff Section (Worked in the Round)

Round 1: ch 1, sc on the top of each row of the rib section, join with a sl st in 1st sc (regular size: 48 sts / small size: 40 sts).
Round 2: ch 3, sk 4 sc (including st at base of ch), petal in next sc, ch 7, petal in same sc as last petal, ch 3, sk 3 sc, sc 1 in next sc, *ch 3, sk 3 sc, [3 trtog, ch 7, 3 trtog] in next sc, ch 3, sk 3 sc, sc 1 in next sc; repeat from * to end, working final sc in 1st sc of previous row.
Round 3: ch 5, sk 2 ch, 3 trtog in next ch, [ch 3, 2 trtog] in top of petal just made, sk [1 petal, 3 ch], *sc 1 in next ch (the 4th of 7ch), ch 3, 8 trtog inserting hook as follows: twice in sc just made, sk [3 ch, 1 petal], insert 3 times in next ch, sk [2 ch, 1 sc, 2 ch], insert 3 times in next ch (8 trtog now complete), [ch 3, 2 trtog] in top of the 8 trtog just made, sk [1 petal, 3 ch]; repeat from * around, ending with sc 1 in 4th of last 7ch, ch 3, 5 trtog inserting hook as follows: twice in sc just made, sk [3 ch, 1 petal], insert 3 times in next ch (5 trtog now complete), join with a sl st into top of 1st petal made.

Round 4: [ch 3, 2 trtog] in top of 1st petal in previous row (same place as sl st in previous row), *ch 3, sk 3 ch, sc 1 in next sc, ch 3, sk 3 ch, [3 trtog, ch 7, 3 trtog] into next st (the top of the 8 trtog of the previous row and the center of the hellebore flower); repeat from * around, ending with ch 3, sk 3 ch, sc 1 in last sc, ch 3, sk 3 ch, 3 trtog into same place as sl st in previous row.
Round 5: ch 7, sc 1 into top of next petal (the 1st petal made in previous row), sl st into next ch, ch 3, 5 trtog inserting hook as follows: twice into base of 3 ch just made, sk [2 ch, sc, 2 ch], insert 3 times in next chain (5 trtog now complete), [ch 3, 2 trtog] into top of the 5 trtog just made, *sk [1 petal, 3 ch], sc 1 in next ch (the 4th of 7ch), ch 3, 8 trtog, inserting hook as follows: twice in the sc just made, sk [3 ch, 1 petal], insert 3 times in next ch, sk [2 ch, 1 sc, 2 ch], insert 3 times in next ch (8 trtog now complete), [ch 3, 2 trtog] in top of the 8 trtog just made; repeat from * around, ending with sk [1 petal, 3 ch], sc 1 in next ch (the 4th of 7ch), [ch 3, 2 trtog] in sc just made, join with a sl st to top of the 5 trtog at the beginning of this row. Fasten off and weave in ends.

If you're a beginner and would like to learn the basic crochet stitches, you can find full instructions on my website: silverpebble.net.

Drawing Feathers

A gray pigeon feather found on an urban street may seem like a common sight and is easily overlooked, but upon close examination, every feather is beautiful. A central quill, or rachis, is lined on both sides by delicate fibers or barbs that have microscopic hooks that interlock to ensure that the feather is able to push air downwards and create lift effectively. Feathers are small pieces of natural engineering, and each one you find has been partly responsible for innumerable flights, which is rather humbling. Recently, I found something truly beautiful in our village wood: a jay's feather. It's rather small and blackish in color, but is hatched with the most vivid kingfisher blue. It is one of my most precious nature finds.

Materials

Paper (anything will do, but thick
   textured paper is ideal)
Your choice of pen, pencil, or ink and brush
Collection of feathers

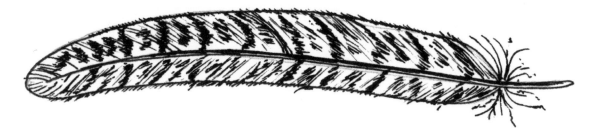

Step by Step

1 Take a good look at your feather in detail. The central quill is the best place to begin. Note how far down it protrudes from the bottom of the fibers or barbs and where the shaft ends. Make a mental note of the curve of the central quill and then begin. Drawing a single line for the quill is perfect for your first attempt—the main aim is not to achieve perfection but to approximate the proportions of your feather.

2 Draw an outline of the fibers or barbs. Capturing the overall shape of the feather is the aim here—again, it does not have to look like a photograph.

3 In two or three areas along the length of the central quill, draw in a few barbs. Odd numbers look especially effective. If the barbs have split from one another in one or two places, draw these triangular gaps and erase the corresponding area of outline.

4 Add any downy or fluffy barbs, if your feather has them, at the base and add an extra line to widen the central quill—close to the original line at the top of the feather and slightly further away towards the quill end to suggest increased thickness.

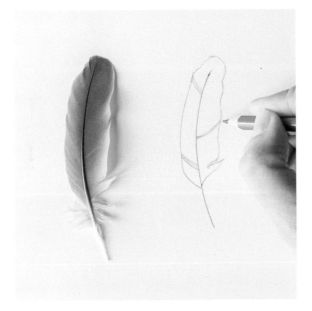

5 That's it! A simple line drawing of a feather. Sit back and bask in your artistic skills. Self-criticism is forbidden. If it looks a little like your dog may have drawn it (as my first feathery attempts did), then remember: wonkiness is beautiful. And practice will help—make a whole collection of feathers while out on walks and keep drawing them. Stylized, simplistic drawings can be just as eye-catching as photographically detailed ones.

Forced Blossoms

Where I live, the appearance of blackthorn or sloe blossom in the hedges is a key sign that the days are getting longer. In mid-February, the buds on the blackthorns begin to show as clusters of tiny pale dots against the dark, almost black bark. The sight of them is hugely uplifting—it marks the beginning of the end of winter and acts as a cue for me to do a special, slightly embarrassing dance. The buds of several other spring blossom trees begin to swell around the same time. In the United Kingdom, forsythia and cherry plum bloom towards the end of February, but there is a way to hasten the appearance of their blossoms, a little. Bringing stems or branches of these species into the warmth of your house can speed up the development and opening of the flowers. If the weather is especially damp and dingy as January ends, the thought of a blossom emerging on your shelf or windowsill in February can be enormously uplifting. It will help ease your way through the final weeks of winter. Encouraging blossoms to open early is surprisingly simple, no matter where you live in the world, and can be attempted with any tree or shrub whose flower buds begin to show in late winter.

Materials

Pruning shears or sturdy scissors
Branches or stems cut from spring-blossoming trees and shrubs with developing buds
Newspaper (optional)
Bathtub filled halfway with warm water (optional)
Vases and jars to display your blossoms

Keep an Eye Out

Blackthorn or sloe (*Prunus spinosa*) grows in Europe, western Asia, and eastern North America. If it doesn't grow near you, simply watch carefully for flower buds to appear on trees and shrubs in your local area. Ask for permission where necessary and cut a few stems. This method works well with developing blossom buds of any species of cherry, plum, or apple tree.

Step by Step

1 Identify trees and shrubs whose buds develop from mid-January onwards. It helps if you make a note of the blossoms growing near your house during the previous spring or the sloes and cherry plums in autumn, as the bare branches and stems can be tricky to identify during winter.

2 Use the pruning shears to cut some branches and stems from the trees and shrubs. Don't cut too many from one plant.

3 You can simply place the stems and branches you've gathered into water and set them in a warm, well-lit spot. Depending on their stage of development when you cut them down, the blossoms should open over the course of the next week or two.

4 To speed up the process even further, fill your bathtub halfway with lukewarm water, wrap your stems and branches in newspaper, and submerge the bundle you have made in the bath. Leave in the warm water for 20–30 minutes, remove the bundle, and unwrap the stems. Bash the cut ends of the stems and branches a little with a large pebble, small hammer, or other heavy object to expose more of the water vessels (xylem) within the stems to the water in the vase.

5 Place the vase in a warm, well-lit spot and your blossoms should emerge in a few days.

6 Gaze happily at the little floral snippets of spring you have brought forward in time.

Lemon, Thyme, and Ginger Bars

During winter and especially in the weeks following the holiday season, citrus fruit is at its best. This is also one of the most common times of year for cold and flu viruses can lurk. There is some evidence that the vitamin C in citrus fruits can help to shorten the duration and severity of colds, and both the fresh ginger and fresh thyme I have included in this recipe contain compounds with proven antiviral and antibacterial properties. Together, all three ingredients not only taste zingy but could also provide a baked defense against wintry ailments.

The combination of the soft, sharp lemon filling with the crisp butteriness of the shortbread crust is sure to brighten any cold, gray afternoon. Along with the plum blondies on page 22, these lemon bars make an excellent snack for a nature walk. Alternatively, eat a large slice warm, straight from the oven, with a dollop of whipped cream or crème fraîche on top, a warm drink, and a favorite audiobook.

Ingredients

For the shortbread crust:
14 tablespoons (200 g) butter, softened
½ cup (110 g) light brown sugar
1⅔ cups (205 g) all-purpose flour
¾ cup (90 g) cornmeal

For the lemon filling:
3 large eggs, lightly whisked
4 lemons, juiced and zested
¾ cup (165 g) light brown sugar
3 tablespoons (25 g) all-purpose flour
2 teaspoons fresh thyme leaves
1 tablespoon fresh ginger, grated

Makes 12–15 bars

Step by Step

1 Line a 9 x 12-inch (22 x 32-cm) or similarly sized square baking pan with parchment paper and preheat your oven to 350°F (180°C).

2 Beat the softened butter and sugar together in a bowl until pale and fluffy—this should take 2–3 minutes.

3 Add the flour and cornmeal, and stir into the creamed butter and sugar until the mixture forms a coherent dough.

4 With your fingers, push the shortbread mixture into your lined baking pan and up the sides to form a uniform layer on the base and around the edge of the pan. This will encase the lemon filling and prevent it from seeping over the edges of the shortbread. Smooth the surface of the dough with the back of a spoon. Bake the shortbread for 15 minutes until just golden. Then set to one side.

5 Place the eggs and lemon juice into a small bowl and beat them together.

6 Add the zest, sugar, and flour for the lemon filling to another bowl with a pouring spout or a large batter bowl and mix together. Make a well in the center, and, using a sieve strain the lemon juice and egg mixture into it while whisking continually until everything is well-combined. Add the ginger and mix to distribute.

7 To prevent the lemon mixture from overflowing over the edge of the shortbread, open your oven, pull out the shelf, and place your baking tray onto it. Pour the lemon mixture into the shortbread crust and gently push the shelf back in. Scatter the thyme leaves on top. Bake for a further 10–15 minutes until just set with a slight wobble.

8 Cut into slices, eat warm, or allow to cool. Enjoy with a cup of tea or add to lunchboxes.

#makingwinter

In November 2015, I started the Instagram hashtag #makingwinter, encouraging folk to share their images of coziness, creativity, and nature. I was keen to create a soothing, uplifting gallery to which anyone could contribute and which would be a source of online creative solace and inspiration to visit on days when winter's gloom may creep in. I continued the project in the winter of 2016–17, and the feed now has an extraordinary collection of beautiful, seasonal photographs. There are shots of snowy landscapes, needlearts, baking, firesides, gardening, and festivities. I'm thrilled that so many Instagrammers have joined forces to create such a brilliant online retreat.

I wanted to share some of them here to show just how lovely the #makingwinter feed is, should you need a little visual solace, and to encourage you to get involved, too. It was tricky to choose favorites—there were so many shots that captured the aim and essence of *Making Winter*—but I managed to narrow my selection down to the eight images shown on the opposite page. Each contributor has brought their own inspiration, subtlety, and a gorgeous range of seasonal creativity to the project. Each of their feeds is a soothing online destination and will make your eyes happy. I thoroughly recommend that you look them up.

Left to right from the top:
@mysuburbanfarm
@lobsterandswan
@helena.moore
@marrbell
@hannahargyle
@gemmakoomen
@illyriapottery
@craftpod.co.uk

Acknowledgments

My husband, Andy, has encouraged me and cheered me on throughout the process of making this book and has brought me innumerable cups of tea while I was balancing on chairs to take pictures of cake or swearing under my breath as I tried to wrestle yarn into three-dimensional berries. He looked after our girls when I was on a deadline and took masses of shots of my hands making things. I'm so grateful. Hugest thanks to him.

My smallish daughters have been so patient while I've been distracted with edits, surrounded by balls of wool, and hunched over a laptop. They have been my most enthusiastic cake tasters, giving each incarnation of the mug cake, the lemon bars, and the streusel cake gleeful marks out of ten. The versions of the recipes that earned 12 out of 10 (or 100 out of 10) are the ones that you read here. My eldest pressed the shutter switch on my camera so many times when my hands were in the shot. She's the best photography assistant.

My agent, Juliet Pickering, listened to my slightly garbled idea about crafting in winter to cheer people up over tea in King's Cross in May 2015 and told me it could become a book. Then, she helped me to make it happen. She has received so many overly giddy emails from me about twigs and cakes and yarn over the past two and half years that I'm sure she must be tired by now. Thank you, Juliet.

Jemima Bicknell has tech edited every crochet pattern in this book. She has been incredibly patient, encouraging and speedy with her edits, and is an astonishing sort of wizard of the wool.

The following women, excellent pals, have been hugely encouraging and inspiring at every stage of this process, telling me I could do it, listening when I felt as though I'd never reach the end and, in Rachael's case, looking after small Mitchells so I could get the book done. They're a very lovely handmade band: Val Curwen, Sue Jones, Helen Ayres, Jane Pink, Fleur Routley, Rachael Ainscough, Charlotte Newland, Jane Duke, Sarah Phelps, and Emma Freud.

Special thanks to Saul Wordsworth, with whom I exchanged hundreds of very silly tweets and who said, on the basis of a load of nonsense about bunions, "You're a writer, you should do a book!" And to the excellent Sarah Dempster, who was my editor for a while and who said the same.

Thank you to the lovely, lovely folk on Twitter and Instagram who were very kind about my photographs and drawings and who egged me on.

Minnie, our dog, has been there by my side through hundreds of hours of photographing and typing. She was always very understanding in the small hours when I was worried about my wreaths.

Contributors and Resources

There are many precious things in the photographs of this book that have been handmade by immensely talented designers and makers. Here are their details should you wish to buy from or commission them.

Sarah Jerath is a potter and made the beautiful mugs, pinch bowls, and plates shown in this book. She digs her own clay out of the ground near her cottage, and her work has a strong sense of place in its body and texture. I cherish the pieces I own that were made by Sarah. Sarah is based near Wigan in the North-West of England. Website: sarahjerath.co.uk.

Loop is the most beautiful shop I have ever stood in. Susan Cropper has created an exquisite collection of skeins of yarn and handmade accessories: it is like the coziest cache of pirate treasure you have ever seen. Even if you don't knit or crochet, a visit to Loop in Camden Passage, London, will lift your day. Oh, and she sells online too. Website: loopknittingshop.com.

Sophie Sellu of **Grain and Knot** carves wooden spoons, knives, and chopping boards by hand. Her work is gorgeously tactile yet functional and appears many times in my photographs here. Sophie is based in London and taught me to carve spoons. Her workshops are excellent. Website: grainandknot.com.

Victoria Magnus of **Eden Cottage Yarns** hand-dyes British fibers and wools in the subtlest of colors in her kitchen sink in Yorkshire. Her skeins are jewel-like and very precious, and I defy you to resist her wooly wares if you encounter them en masse at a yarn show. Her work is gorgeous. Website: edencottagyarns.co.uk.

Metal Clay sells silver clay and all the tools you may need to make your silver fossil pendant. Shayna, Jade, Stuart, and the team are so supportive of new jewelery makers. Website: metalclay.co.uk.

Spoilt Rotten Beads are another of my silver clay suppliers. Juliet and the team are incredibly helpful. Website: spoiltrottenbeads.co.uk.

About the Author

Emma Mitchell is a popular designer–maker, craft teacher, and naturalist. She lives in a tiny village on the edge of the Cambridgeshire Fens, where she runs nature-inspired craft workshops and creative winter retreats. Emma has been published in the *Guardian*, *Mollie Makes*, *Country Living*, and Kirstie Allsopp's book *Craft*. She's also the creator and editor of *Mollie Makes Comic Relief Crafternoon* magazine, which has raised £100,000 so far for projects in the United Kingdom and Africa. She shares her joy of craft and her daily nature observations on her Instagram account, @silverpebble2, and her Twitter feed, @silverpebble. She blogs at silverpebble.net.